WORDS TO THE SILENCE: A BOOK OF UNCOMMON PRAYER

by Schuyler Rhodes

with illustrations by Frances Harkness

DEDICATION:

This effort is dedicated to my wife Lisa, whose support, nurture and encouragement have made this and so many other things possible; and to the wonderful Christian community at Washington Square United Methodist Church.

WORDS TO THE SILENCE:

A Book of Uncommon Prayer

by Schuyler Rhodes

ISBN 1-877871-74-5
Educational Ministries, Inc.
165 Plaza Drive
Prescott, AZ 86303
800-221-0910

TABLE OF CONTENTS

This book is organized after the fashion of an Order of Worship Service.

VII - Page 69 - **Eucharistic Prayers**. Sharing Holy Communion each week is key to the depth and authenticity of spirituality which is in process at our church. More than an act of memory, more than a simple meal, it bonds the people of God together in hope and unity around the sacred table.

VIII - Page 75 - **Hymns for a New Church.** Familiar hymns have been given new words to express the excitement of a new vision of being the Church in the world.

IX - Page 87 - **Rites of the Church**. Here are services for New Members, Commissioning a Mission Delegation, Marriage and Baptism.

X - Page 105 - **Stories: Reclaiming an Ancient Tradition.** These illustrations are designed for discussion, preaching and community interaction.

FORWARD

ASKING QUESTIONS, SEEKING SOLUTIONS

If one takes the time to listen, it's easy to hear a buzz of anxious questioning throughout the church. There are echoes and shouts, sobs and whispers, and even at times, a chuckle or two. Some of it is reasoned, careful, and founded in prayer. Some gently prods and cajoles. Some careens dangerously toward ideology, stretching our connection and our affection. Some sinks into despair and cynicism. And some questions are even seized as an opportunity for joy and new life.

Whatever form these queries take, they can be easily distilled into a singular concern. How are we to revitalize our church? How can we claim a sense of vision and power which seems to be increasingly elusive?

Elusive indeed. In an ever more secular world, religious motivation is increasingly suspect. Instead of the stately, august presence of people like Ralph Stockman, Frances McConnel and Georgia Harkness, church people must now make do with the partisan bickering of left versus right, while televangelists of questionable moral character are trotted out as the voice of our faith. The traditional church, with empty pews and buildings rented out to everyone from day care centers to methadone clinics, is paying a price for bungled and agenda-laden theologies. The people, it seems, have voted with their feet, and left the church scrambling to figure out its mistakes in the background of history's dusky shadows.

REMEMBERING OUR STORY....

Looking at early Christianity, we see that this isn't the first time the church has been in trouble. In days gone by, our ancestors in the faith suffered persecution, division, and a frequently less than sympathetic society. Over the years, the church has been forced underground on numerous occasions. Christians were sent to the Roman arenas where, ironically, the first pipe organs were used to drown out the cries of hapless martyrs. They went also to gas chambers and prisons. Times for the church, to say the least, have been difficult before this.

History is a good reminder that then, as now, there are no single easy answers to the complex issues which face people of faith. Would that it were so.

Yet in this instance, the words to an old Beatles song, "Yellow Submarine," come close to the beginnings of an answer as it sings out, "Everyone of us is all we need." And indeed, the solution for our fading faith institutions will be discovered, not in ideological jaunts to the right or left, not in up or down, or in any other divisionistic grasping. It will be found, if God wills it, in the sacred variety of gifts and graces possessed by all the children of God who claim the name of Christ. Each person, each pastor, each congregation will need to both listen and speak, to offer and receive as we remake the grand puzzle of our common life in a new century.

PRAYER AND THE NEW CHURCH

For my part, one avenue to renewal is through worship. Worship is a key element of who we are as a people. It is the moment of our most public pronouncement about who we are and to whom we belong. What we do together when we stop to pray and praise God each week is intimately connected to the rest of our Christian life. It is the hub of our wheel of faith, with spokes emanating out into our lives and the lives of all we touch. As such, the service of worship witnesses to the energy and power of the love of God in Jesus Christ. At its best, Christian worship is incarnational, embodying God's relentless and unlimited love in song and praise. It is joyful, somber, ecstatic, sorrowful, open, loving, and even at times, divinely silly.

It is in the worship experience that the people of God find their center in Christ. It is in worship that the foundation stones for authentic Christian community are laid. And it is in worship that the mission of the Church is articulated.

At Washington Square United Methodist Church, we have worked together to renew the Christian experience through worship. It is not, as Paul would remind us in Philippians, that we have already gotten there. But we have made a start. With music, drama, dance, preaching and prayers, the community has taken the worship experience and reinvented it for a 21st century church. From the introduction of a jazz liturgy, to celebrating Holy Communion each week, to writing original prayers keyed to the life of the community, and involving lay folk intimately in the process, we have endeavored to give birth to a worship experience which is inspiring and transforming.

We remain, like all communities, people who struggle with all of the daily realities of being a church in the world. We stumble, err, and continue on what our founder, John Wesley would name as the "way to perfection," working out our salvation "in fear and trembling."

Yet in all our imperfection, it is safe to say that we have found a deep and abiding intimacy in Christ through our worship life together. And it is this intimacy which has empowered our church for growth and ministry.

Just as worship alone is not the key to revitalizing the church, neither are the prayers enclosed here, the only answer for worship. They are merely reflections of Christian lives at prayer in the context of a specific community. The reader is invited to use these in worship and in private prayer. It's also hoped that these prayers will be changed, rewritten and adapted to fit the needs of churches who, like Washington Square United Methodist Church, are seeking new life in Christ and in community through worship.

Washington Square United Methodist Church Faith Declaration & Mission Statement

We declare ourselves to be
a people of faith: a people who claim
God's Creative rule as the power in our lives
above and beyond the power of governments and social categories.
We believe that the will of God is life.
We reject weapons as a murderous protection
which take food and sustenance from our brothers and sisters.
Together we lift up our vision of God
and of God's Shalom as our only true security.
As one people we choose joyfully
to embrace life as God's will.
And with Jesus, our Christ,
we stand in solidarity with the poor, the oppressed,
the forgotten children of Creation.
With our fingers in our blooded hands and sides,
we confess our faith and declare that:
The Spirit of God is upon us
Because God has anointed us
to preach good news to the poor,
God has sent us to proclaim release to the captives
and recovery of sight to the blind;
to set at liberty
those who are oppressed;
to proclaim the acceptable year of our God. ✠

ABOUT THESE PRAYERS

Each week as I sit to contemplate the coming Sunday morning service, I begin by leaning back in my chair and closing my eyes. In the purpled blackness, the citied sounds of this place swirl around me. Kids from the Day Care Center dance about, singing a song about Martin Luther King, Jr.; some church members mill about in the outer office, deciding when to plan the next outing for the Covenant Discipleship Group, while others make calls for our homeless shelter and wonder about the anthem for next Sunday. My secretary negotiates with a couple of street folks, and my wife knocks on the office door to tell me that it's time for our afternoon walk. All of these sounds meld together into something startlingly like the grace of God.

And in this glorious swirling of community life I cannot help but feel a humble kind of joy. I wonder how it is that I came to be the one to bring the Word of God each week to this community; how it could possibly fall on me to provide a worship experience that would be healing, transforming and inspiring?

Then I open my eyes, and I begin to write. The prayers for worship emerge from a sense of who we are as a community. They come also out of our common vision of a church called to renew and revitalize the ministry of Christ in this place. In each prayer there is something which speaks to our process, our lives together.

The Centering Prayer, on this particular Sunday, comes from a long discussion with one church member who has a hard time pushing away the voices of her world so she can enter into the worship experience. It is specific. It is clear. It speaks, not only to her, but to all who must sort out the din of voices pulling at their heart strings and demanding allegiance we would rather give to God.

The Prayer for the Church calls on all of us to accept the call to lead our Annual Conference as the ones who will speak the prophetic words of the Gospel, and to some who would rather not hear them. It mentions our new Bishop and the special call we have as an urban church. This too speaks of specific context and mission. As I write, I find that these prayers come also from my own prayer life and from the depth of our Bible studies and covenant prayer groups within the community. These words are, as the concept of "liturgy" suggests, the work of the people.

There is nothing wrong with "canned" liturgies that come from hymnals and books of worship. They are carefully wrought and full of good suggestions. They also contain historic and traditional creeds and prayers which are a significant part of our common identity. But they cannot, by their nature, speak specifically to the ongoing faith life of a congregation. That is why liturgical renewal must be accompanied, at least in part, by original prayers and confessions written and designed for the specific community who will be sharing in them.

These prayers are from the life of a wonderful small church in New York City. We are a United Methodist Church, rooted deeply in scripture and in our Wesleyan heritage. Yet we also have a unique heritage and personality of our own. We are a family, and these are our family utterances of hope, our confessions, and our prayers of joy.

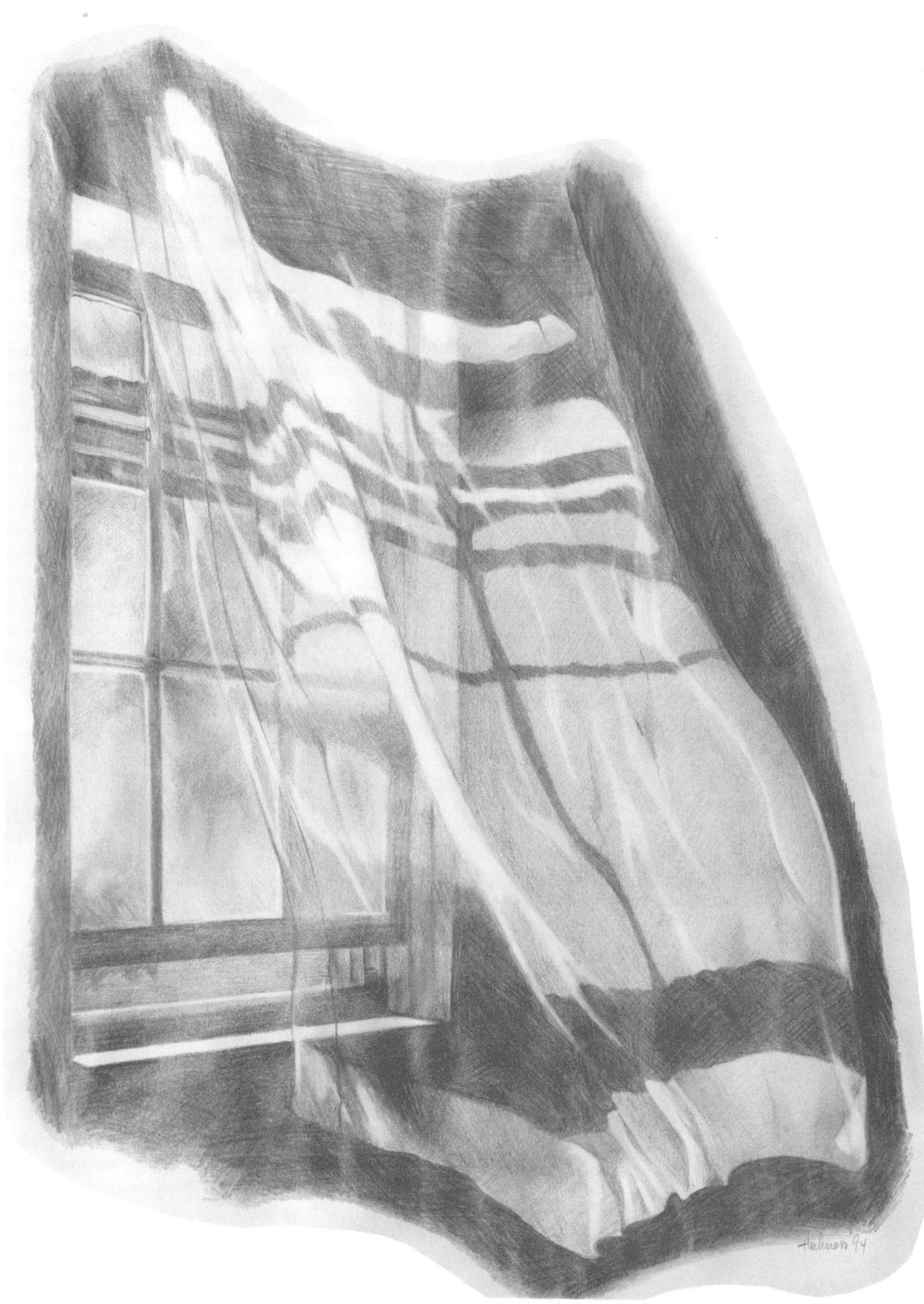

CENTERING PRAYERS

The music begins. Strains of a familiar hymn, laced with virtuoso jazz harmonies, draw the chattering crowd on the steps slowly into the sanctuary. Looking around at peeling paint and partially restored walls, the small congregation moves gradually from eager greetings and hugs into meditative prayer as they prepare for worship. These prayers are for the time when community moves from getting to church, to being in worship together.

1

Loving Breath who draws me to this place, still my soul and open my heart to the power of Your spirit. Soothe my anxious thoughts and pour the healing waters of Your compassion over my weariness. I need Your loving, God. Let this hour be the door that I seek, and let this community be the key. In the name of the Risen One, I pray, Amen.

2

Loving Spirit, in this hour of praise and unity, teach me a new song. Open my heart to the steadfast love and faithfulness that mark Your presence in all things. Awaken me to the joy of Your way in the world, and turn me from the nightmare of cynicism and anger; loneliness and despair. Amen.

3

Holy Spirit, come and dwell within me. Touch me with the joy of Your presence and fill me with the power of Your love. For now is the time of celebration; the revealing of Your way of being. Amen.

4

Strong and Gentle God, voice of my hope, as we move into the community life this day of worship and praise, grant that my heart and eyes will be open to receive all people in Your name. Remove fear and doubt from our midst, and build the foundations of trust and solidarity with the fire of Your love. This is my prayer and my dream, in the name of life and wholeness, Amen.

5

Holy One who sustains and nurtures, pour Your spirit upon me now. Unlock my heart and open my arms to receive the loving embrace of Your power. Amen.

6

Creating and loving God, now is the moment in my life when I have stopped moving long enough to listen to the quiet, overwhelming power of Your voice. In the echoes of Your call to ministry and service my heart stretches like a kitten in the sun to warm itself. Grant in this hour that I may find the strength in prayer and community to grow in Your presence. I am grateful, humble, and ready God. Amen.

7

Comforting breath, whose presence seeps in and around me, I ask now for a unity of heart and mind. Wash over me and knit the warring pieces of self into one focused garment —seamless—whole. Plow through me so that the movement of my spirit becomes one with You in the living of these days. Amen.

8

Holy One, find me now, as the dust of my life settles in this moment of peace. Touch my heart and free it from the chains of grief and pain. Heal me, Loving Spirit, and hold the sum of me in the flowing ease of Your being. Amen.

9

God of hope and healing, breathe the power of Your love into my wounded and weary soul. Unlock the doors of my heart and let me drink from the bottomless well of Your embracing Spirit. Touch me. Fill me. Renew me God, and lead me in the ways of Your justice and Your peace. For now is the time of my faithfulness. Amen.

10

As I sit quietly God, breathing slowly and centering my heart, I begin to sense the stillness that I know to be Your presence. As the world's flood of apprehension and fear falls gently from my heart, I can hear Your voice calling me from the bondage of this world to wander in the desert in search of hope and justice. But the desert is hot and dry, and I am afraid. I do not believe, down deep, that You will wander with me, and I long for proof of Your fidelity. Open my eyes and my heart, healing presence, and help me know that You are always and ever present as we offer our prayers for each other and our community, grant us all the vulnerability that we know so well through Jesus: the vulnerability of love and compassion. Amen.

11

Loving and Gentle God, as the world bristles with weapons and fear, I sink into my seat feeling the sweat of despair on my brow. It is the fear, oh God, which halts, paralyzes and destroys. It is the fear which drives us apart from each other, and from You. In these halting, brittle moments, my prayer is a healing prayer. I pray that Your presence in me and in the world will reach out and grow in compassion, hope and power so that this disease of fear and violence will melt away into the light of love and justice. Amen.

12

Gentle and Loving Friend, there are so many expectations and demands swirling around me as I enter into this moment of worship. Help me to stop my striving long enough to feel the touch of Your embrace in my life. Teach me the long slow sigh that makes room in my heart for the wonder of Your love. And lift me up, God of my days, in newness and in hope so that I may find the reality of new life in Your presence. Amen.

13

Great and Gracious God, find me in this moment and center my heart so that I might receive the healing power of Your love in my life. Unbind my wounds so that the healing breath of Your spirit might touch them. Open my heart, my ears, and my arms so that I might be one in community, in hope, in love. Amen.

14

Great Spirit who binds us together, blow Your loving breeze into our hearts this day as we gather to praise the reality of Your presence in our lives. Warm us with the summer wind of Your compassion and open our hearts to the joyful justice task You lay before us. In hope, in laughter, in sorrow, in laughter, and in wonder we pray, Amen.

15

Wondrous and Gentle Spirit who calls creation into wholeness, find me now in this quiet moment. Center my heart and open me to Your loving power, so that my being might be a witness to the love that You manifest in Jesus. Grant me vulnerability and openness so that I may move and sway in the winds of Your Spirit. Amen.

16

Loving Spirit, I come today to wait on the power of Your spirit. In these moments of gathering and prayer, the weight of my own wanderings begins to fall to the openness of Your forgiving grace. Kindle my heart for new beginnings, O God, and may the mighty wind of Your spirit fan these glowing embers into a burning faith for the ministry of this community. In hope and struggle, I offer my prayer, Amen.

17

Healing and Liberating God, touch me with the power of Your spirit. Soothe the tired, aching lines in my face and fill me with an awareness of Your presence and Your grace. Renew me in the depth of Your Creating Love. Open my eyes to the possibilities for change and growth in my life and in the life of the world. Open my heart so that I may embrace the struggles of Your people and make them my own. And God, stretch out my hands so that I clasp the hands of sisters and brothers near and far. In the hope of healing and liberation for the whole of Creation, I offer myself through this prayer, Amen.

18

O Loving God, source of all life,it is an almost hesitant joy that finds me in prayer. I know that the tomb is empty; that new life is not only possible, but present and flourishing all around me. Yet the truth is that I am afraid to believe it. I am on uncertain ground, and do not want this vision to disappear. Hold me, Savior God. Grasp my hand and speak my name as the gardener spoke to Mary. Help me hear Your voice calling me forth into the resurrection life and teach me the unrestrained and wild joy of new life in You. In the name of the risen and Living Christ, I pray with these words and with my life, Amen.

19

Spirit of Hope, flow into us and fill us with Your power. Recover in us a vision of love and justice which will spill over the dividing walls between us with an abundance of joy. Amen.

20

Wonderful God who comes so that we might all have life, surround us now and link our hearts into one. Create in us a spirit of wholeness, a longing for justice, and a joy in the struggling. We ask it in Jesus' name, Amen.

21

Loving Spirit, the wind of Your compassion blows 'round my heart and the sense of Your presence calms me. As the time of our worship begins, open my heart to the beauty of Your power in the world, and grant that with this community, I may find the newness of life that flows among us now. Amen.

22

Strong and Gentle God, in this hour there is a place for me to sit and claim the love You hold out for me. There is a moment; a quiet space for me to know that there is nothing that can come between me and the overwhelming reality of Your love. And though I get tired, frustrated, and angry, though the world grabs me and pulls me along in its frenzied whirling way, I know that here and now, You are with me. Touch me. Heal me. Hold me in the arms of Your compassion, and renew me with the breath of Your spirit. In Christ's name I pray, Amen.

23

Holy God, in the rush and confusion that so often marks my life, I find myself longing for something which seems to move and dance away as I strain to watch and listen. The strain has wearied me, and I am tired. In this hour, Gracious One, my hope is for a calming of my heart and the freeing of my spirit so that I may receive the Call; the yearning You have for my life. Help me, God, so that I may hear You. Amen.

24

Holy and Creating God, hold my heart and quiet my spirit in this hour of praise and worship. Send the healing power of Your spirit upon me and open me to the wonders of Your love in this community and in the world. Amen.

25

Loving God, it is in this moment that I grasp the overwhelming reality of the sacrifice You made in giving Your child to me as Savior and Redeemer. In this hour, healing Master, let me feel Your presence within me so that the Christ who was crucified, and is crucified still in gutters and alleyways around the world may find His rising in the healing power of my transformed life. Send Your spirit into this, my community, so that together we may be the embodiment of the love You gave us in Jesus. For it is in His name that I offer this prayer. Amen.

26

God of our lives, find us now, we pray. Touch the heart of our community with the love that makes all things new; the love that insists on healing; the love which is the reality of Your presence, here and now. Claim us as Your own, Loving Spirit, and live in us so that we may bear the fruits of justice and love. In Christ's name we pray, Amen.

27

O Gracious and Gentle Master, we gather this evening as ones who seek Your will in our lives. Together we open our hearts and still our rushing spirits so that we may hear Your voice in the darkness. Bind us up and heal us, Loving Parent, and grant us the courage to face the power of vulnerable love, the love of Your child, Jesus. For it is in His name that we pray, Amen.

28

Spirit of love and hope, God of sorrow and wasted dreams, it's morning, and I rise to seek Your presence in my life. The search seems so long, and at times even pointless. And finally, I arrive here tired and spent, yearning for the power of Your touch. Hold me, Sovereign of my days, and teach me the reality of Your presence in all places and all times. Fill me with Your strength and walk with me on this journey so that I may be a living witness to the truth of Your love and compassion. Amen.

29

Loving God, I sit here in the quiet, knowing of conflict and brokenness in my life. Around me there is contention and disharmony; anger and pain. And as the hour of praise draws near, I ask that You come, Holy Spirit. Come as the wind in the trees and fill me with the power of Your love. Build in me a trust and confidence that heals and seeks reconciliation. Come, sacred breath, and breathe into my heart the ways of life and wholeness so that I may journey with You, even as You are a part of me. Amen.

30

Find me now, as the dust of my life settles in this moment of peace. Touch my heart and free it from the chains of grief and pain. Heal me, Loving Spirit, and hold the sum of me in the flowing ease of Your being. Amen.

31

Healing God who fills the spaces in my brokenness, flow into me and rekindle my spirit. Bind up my wounds and create within me a wholeness which feeds on the power of Your love. Amen.

32

O Loving God, source of all life, it is an almost hesitant joy that finds me in prayer. I know that the tomb is empty; that new life is not only possible, but present and flourishing all around me. Yet the truth is that I am afraid to believe it. I am on uncertain ground, and do not want this vision to disappear. Hold me Savior God. Grasp my hand and speak my name as the gardener spoke to Mary. Help me to hear Your voice calling me forth into the resurrection life, and teach me the unrestrained and wild joy of new life in You. In the name of the risen and living Christ, I pray with these words and with my life, Amen.

33

Come, Holy Spirit and renew Your creation. Come, Holy Spirit, and renew my weary heart. Come, Holy Spirit, flow among us and make us bold in love and joyous in singing. Amen.

34

God of Love, this is a season of the heart. It is a time of penitence, a time of reflection and prayer. In these hours and days, Holy Spirit, create in me a new way of seeing, a new way of being in this world which You created for love, for wholeness, and for life ongoing. I ask this in hope, in wonder and in the surpassing joy of knowing that Jesus Christ is Lord, Amen.

35

Loving and Gentle God, I come into this sanctuary hoping that it is named so in truth as well as tradition. As my heart grows still and the power of Your Spirit fills me, I am grateful for the power of Your presence. As I join this community in worship, help me to give myself to the reality of Your yearning for my life. Guide me. Touch me. Heal me. In the name of the Child I pray, Amen.

36

Gentle and Loving God, You bring me time and again to moments of knowing the truth of You. In this hour I pray that I might again discover You in the midst of this worshipping community. Let my will be Yours, Holy friend. Liberate my spirit, and grant as we join together in worship that we may see past the bound up and broken face of an institution to the fresh and bubbling wellspring of our common heart in Christ Jesus. Awaken in us the child-like joy of being Your community, renew our hearts for ministry as Your people. In love and power I offer my prayer, Amen.

CALLS TO WORSHIP

As Christians, we know that the voice of God calls ever and always to us. We are Called to serve, to suffer, to laugh, and to dance. And we are Called, as well, to be worshiping people, moving together into a common life that is itself and act of worship.

37

Leader: This is a day to celebrate new life!
People: We come to celebrate the reality of this new life!
Leader: We come to embrace the resurrection life!
People: For it is in Christ that we are made new.
Leader: It is in Christ that the dividing walls of our hostility fall away and we come together in wholeness and joy!
People: No longer male or female, slave or free, gay or straight, black or white, but one people: bound in Christ's liberating love!
ALL: Together in this hour, let us join as one body with one voice to proclaim our joy in praise, worship, and song. Amen.

38

Leader: We are called into community as ones who stand for life!
People: We are called into lives of hope.
Leader: The voice we hear is the voice of our longing;
People: The cry of our hearts.
Leader: It is the voice of a God whose name is Love,
People: A God, whose will is justice.
ALL: In prayer and song, we respond to the call of this God, and offer ourselves and all that we are for the healing of the world. Amen.

39

Leader: Holy is our God!
People: Our God is a lover of justice,
Leader: Our God establishes equity and wholeness.
People: Come, let us worship this God.
ALL: Let us go together to God's Holy mountain in praise and song! Amen.

40

Leader: We come to open our hearts in praise and hope!
People: We rise in praise of the God of love!
Leader: This God strengthens us, and blesses the children within us.
People: This God calls us to be peacemakers both in word and deed.
ALL: We come to embrace the Spirit in hope and to worship in praise and thanks. Amen. *(from Psalm 147)*

41

Leader: This is the day our God has made!
People: Let us rejoice and be glad in it!
Leader: For we are God's people!
People: The work of the Creator's hands.
Leader: As God's people we are called in faith to be the light of the world.
People: To be the light in places where there is no vision,
Leader: To be the light in places of pain and sorrow,
People: To be the light of renewal and liberation for the church and for the world.
Leader: Together we bind our hearts in worship and praise to experience God's yearning for us.
People: Together, we draw strength and power from the reality of this Holy community.
ALL: Together, we lift up the cross and move forward in joy and struggle. Amen.

42

Leader: Sing to God a new song!
People: We sing of God's victory in the world.
Leader: In the wake of this victory, we rejoice as one people.
People: This is a victory gained not with weapons or with fear,
but with hope and struggle in partnership with a loving God.
Leader: This is the victory of life over death, of joy over grief;
People: This is the victory of lives together in loving community.
ALL: Let us sing the new song! Amen.

43

Leader: This is what God has spoken: Keep justice and righteousness,
People: For soon my salvation will come, and my deliverance will be revealed.
Leader: All who hold fast to my covenant, these will I bring to my holy mountain,
People: And make them joyful in my house of prayer.
Leader: Their burnt offerings and their sacrifices will be accepted on my altar,
People: For my house shall be called a house of prayer for all peoples!

44

Leader: A mighty wind has blown,
People: And tongues of fire have danced!
Leader: The presence of the Spirit is with us,
People: Just as the Christ promised.
Leader: The presence of the Spirit moves and gathers us into community.
People: The Spirit moves us to lives of nurturing and challenging one another,
celebrating and witnessing to the truth which we name as Love in the world.
Leader: Let us marvel at God's power,
People: God's power at work in and through us! Amen.

Leader: We are a people of God!
People: Our hearts are called into healing and compassion!
Leader: Our lives, too, are named in this call.
People: And in faith, we respond.
Leader: In hope, we stand firm.
People: For we know that the spirit of God is upon us.
Leader: God has anointed us to bring good news to the poor.

People: God sends us to proclaim release to the captives,
Leader: Recovery of sight to the blind,
People: To set at liberty those who are oppressed.
ALL: To proclaim God's acceptable year in our hearts, our lives, and in our world. Amen.

45

Leader: We are a people called out by God.
People: We gather now in joy and anticipation to hear this call.
Leader: We are a people caught up in a world that would silence the voice of God's yearning for us.
People: Still, we gather.
Leader: We are a people in struggle, trying to claim our heritage, trying to claim our church.
People: And it is from this struggle that we emerge; hopeful, fearful and ready.
ALL: Amen!

46

Leader: Together we come to hear a voice crying in the wilderness.
People: Prepare the way of our God!
Leader: Every valley shall be filled,
People: Every mountain and hill shall be brought low,
Leader: The crooked shall be made straight.
ALL: And we shall see it together! Amen!

47

Leader: As a people of faith, we are called to journey together!
People: This church, this community, is the starting place for this journey .
Leader: So while we come this day, in praise and adoration, to worship our God,
People: We hear the voice of the Christ sending us into the world.
ALL: We come together now in a spirit of worship and gladness to praise God and to gain the nurture for our journey together as the people of God. Amen.

48

Leader: The hand of God rests upon this community.
People: We will be a shelter, a present help in the midst of the storm.
Leader: Our God is present!
People: God's healing and liberation will flow from us!
Leader: We are the good community of the Loving God!
All: In hope, in joy, in struggle and in certainty, we move with the rhythmic breath of the Holy Spirit—to pray—to love—to work. Amen.

49

Leader: Come, Holy Spirit!
People: Blow into our lives and ignite us as Your people in the world!
Leader: Speak to us in the tongues of Your liberating love
People: And teach us the language of Your compassion.
ALL: Come Holy Spirit! Renew us and claim us for the living of these days! Amen.

50

Leader: We are called, like Moses, from the fire of a burning bush.
People: The voice echoes around our hearts and we are drawn close to the flame.
Leader: But something stops us...something stills our hand.
People: We would rather that someone else were called: someone more talented, someone with more skills or time.
Leader: But no, it is we who are called.
People: It is to us that God extends the gift of ministry and the hope of healing and liberation for the human community.
ALL: With a common heart let us draw closer to God's burning bush and accept our calling. Let us worship our God in song and in prayer, in the reality of our very lives. Amen.

51

Leader: We come to open our hearts in praise and hope!
People: We rise in praise of the God of love!
Leader: This God strengthens us, and blesses the children within us.
People: This God calls us to be peacemakers both in word and deed.
ALL: We come to embrace the Spirit in hope and to worship in praise and thanks. Amen. *(from Psalm 147)*

52

Leader: Ours is a faith which flows as a river!
People: It is a river whose waters fail not,
Leader: Whose source is the Creating God,
People: Our Redeemer and our Rock.
Leader: We claim the power of the God of Life over the principalities and powers who even now position themselves to deal death to the people, death to the nations, death to God's Creation.
People: We choose life over death, and stand as a people of faith to be counted.
ALL: With one voice and one heart let us join in worship and praise as we celebrate the loving power of our sovereign, our God. Amen.

53

Leader: Sing to God a new song!
People: We sing of God's victory in the world.
Leader: In the wake of this victory, we rejoice as one people.
People: This is a victory gained not with weapons or with fear, but with hope and struggle in partnership with a loving God.
Leader: This is the victory of life over death, of joy over grief;
People: This is the victory of lives together in loving community.
ALL: Let us sing the new song! Amen.

54

Leader: This is the day that God has made!
People: Let us come together in gladness and hope.
Leader: We are God's people,

People: The work of the Creator's hands.
ALL: Claim us, Loving God, even as we claim You now in song and praise!Amen.

55

Leader: We are a people of God,
People: We are a people who come in search of God's vision for us.
Leader: In this time of preparation,
People: In this time of penitence,
Leader: May we focus the power of our faith,
People: May we give freedom to the yearning of our hearts,
ALL: And may we emerge together in the liberating love of our God.

56

Leader: Let us give thanks to God!
People: We gather today to call on God's name.
Leader: Let us speak of God's presence among us!
People: We come to sing and tell of God's Creating Love.
Leader: As children of One Holy Parent, we have gathered.
People: As sisters and brothers in faith, we are joined as one.
ALL: Let the voices of our mouths and the meditations of our hearts be acceptable in Your sight, O God our Redeemer and our Rock. Amen.

57

Leader: Not to us, O God, not to us!
People: But to Your name give glory!
Leader: Why should the nations call upon their gods?
People: Why should we seek idols of silver or gold?
Leader: These are the work of human hands.
People: They cannot speak, or hear, or feel.
Leader: The same is true of their makers.
People: Our God is not a god of metal or cloth.
Leader: Our God is the Creating and Healing God,

People: The nurturing One who comes among us!
ALL: With one voice, let us turn from the gods of the nations and worship the God of life! Amen. *(adapted from Psalm 115)*

58

Leader: Like the sun that is far away, yet close at hand to warm us,
People: So it is that God's Spirit is ever present and around us.
Leader: We shall let no clouds of depression or doubt keep the waves of God's Living Spirit from us.
People: We open now the windows of our souls!
Leader: Come, Creator God, into the core of our being.
ALL: May our worship and the whole of our lives move and have our source in You. Amen.

59

Leader: This is the day of celebration!
People: This is the day we claim God's power in our lives!
Leader: Today, waving palms and singing, we give our allegiance to God's Love.
People: With one voice, we embrace the Love who walks among us, who even now sits on a colt and eyes the city.
Leader: With one heart, we cry Hosanna!
People: Blessed is the One who comes in the name of the Lord. Amen.

60

Leader: Holy is our God!
People: Our God is a lover of justice,
Leader: Our God establishes equity and wholeness.
People: Come, let us worship this God.
ALL: Let us go together to God's Holy mountain in praise and song! Amen.

61

Leader: We are the people of God!

People: We are called in love and compassion into lives that are an act of worship to our Creator.

Leader: In this hour we reach out to touch and be healed by the Holy Spirit as It moves among us.

ALL: Come Holy Spirit, come! Teach us the ways of Your power, and draw us into the reality of being Your church in the world. Amen.

62

Leader: Right now we gather at the foot of the Cross.

People: Right now we know the reality of pain,

Leader: We sense the depth of sorrow.

People: We feel emptiness and finality.

Leader: In this moment we are in the crowd as Jesus is crucified.

ALL: In this moment we pray and sing of broken legs and wounded sides. In this moment, the dance of dying winds like a burial cloth around our hearts. Amen.

63

Leader: Like the rain that falls on the waiting earth, we come to receive God's Holy Spirit!

People: We seek an openness that will bring us growth, change, and wholeness.

Leader: And in our search we are nourished by the reality of God's presence in our midst.

People: For we know that God's realm does not hide in clouds or signs of the times.

Leader: We know that the realm is here awaiting our embrace, in joy and wonder!

ALL: As one people, we gather now to receive the Spirit and to claim our power as the children of God! Amen.

64

Leader: We are gathered as children of the Creating God!
People: Together, we arrive to create and recreate the living tapestry of our faith.
Leader: We are "Ecclesia," those who are called out...
People: We are called out in love and solidarity, compassion and hope to proclaim both the possibility and the reality of new life in our midst.
Leader: We are one; a unity formed not of conformity, but of the strength of our diversity.
ALL: As one people, we gather now in revival and celebration! Amen.

65

Leader: Come, let us discover the reality of God in our lives!
People: We know that God is here in our midst!
Leader: We know that God flows among us as a river, healing, loving, and reconciling.
People: God is a truth that lives, grows, and creates all things new.
ALL: As one people, we gather now to open our hearts to the currents of this Holy River so that we may be nourished as co-creators with our God! Amen!

66

Leader: As a community of God, we gather to claim the power of God's love in our lives.
People: We come to witness to the healing reality of that love as we stand together in worship and praise.
Leader: For we know that without love, we wander and fall—
People: Without love, the vision fails—
ALL: But with the love of God, we find wholeness and peace in the diversity of this community. And it is with this love that we find each other today. Amen.

67

Leader: As the children of God, we claim a unity of love, spirit and hope!
People: Our unity emerges from the lives we share with each other and with our sisters and brothers.
Leader: It is the common life of the Spirit;

People: A life in ministry and service.
Leader: With one voice, let us embrace this life!
ALL: With one heart, let us worship the God who nurtures and holds us as we move forward together! Amen.

68

Leader: We come as a people called out in faith!
People: We come seeking wholeness and community!
Leader: For us, the methods, techniques and tricks of knowing give way in the face of a disarming and self-giving love.
People: It is the love of Christ.
Leader: It is the love of God.
ALL: And in this hour, we join as one to claim and to share this love as our own. For we are certain that neither death nor life, nor angels, nor princi palities, nor things present, nor things to come, nor powers, nor height, nor depth, nor anything else in all Creation will be able to separate us from the love of God in Christ Jesus. Amen.

69

Leader: We are a people created in love!
People: We are born in each moment to be as children in the world.
Leader: We are God's children,
People: The work of Creating hands,
Leader: And we gather now to answer the call to become co-creators with our God.
People: We come to claim our heritage as partners with God, the doing of justice and the making of peace.
ALL: With one voice, we gather to link arms and hearts in our song of love and justice! Amen!

70

Leader: Christ is risen!
People: Christ is risen indeed!
Leader: On this day, we stand triumphant before the world to claim the power of life over death.
People: We gather before an empty tomb to proclaim life,
Leader: To lift up the certainty that death is not the end,
People: To sing with joy that death is not the answer.

Leader: We know that life, love and wholeness are the answers and the way of a loving God who calls us all from the tomb.

ALL: In the name of this God, and in the certainty of new life, we come in praise and joy. Amen!

PRAYERS OF CONFESSION

The notion of confession, over the years, has become ossified into a list of mistakes and vague errors mumbled in rote each Sunday. Though we cannot shy away from our mistakes and stumbling, confession is more than this. It is not one thing, but a combination of the many elements of faith.

Confession has to do with clearly stating who we are and to whom we belong. In the early Church, believers "Confessed" that Jesus Christ was their Sovereign Lord and Savior. The "Confessing Church" of Germany in the 1930s "confessed" its unwavering allegiance to God instead of the Nazi Party.

In Confession, each Christian strives for the opening of hearts that are broken and wounded so that anger and pain can flow out into the light of God's grace and forgiveness.

In confessing prayer, the Christian community takes down the isolating walls built for protection and safety, and steps forth from vulnerability into the healing reality of the grace of God in Christ Jesus.

71

O God of love and justice, we live as a people caught in a storm. Around us rage the powers of anger and violence, the floods of rage and fear. Around us grows a reality that would claim our allegiance and our love. It is not easy to weather the storms, O God, and too often we find ourselves caught up in their fury. We begin to take on anger and frustration, and we participate in the brokenness and suffering which surround us. Forgive us, God of love. Have mercy on us for our unbending spirits and our willful ways. Forgive us, God of justice. Touch us with the newness of life we have in You, and create in us the power to declare Your justice with our lives. For in truth, it is You we claim as Sovereign, and it is to You that we give allegiance—now and always in the name of Christ, Amen.

72

(A Litany)

Leader:	We are part of a world full of words.
People:	So much talk, so little said.
Leader:	As a people, our hearts wilt under the onslaught of these words, and we grow tired.
People:	So much talk, so little done.
Leader:	It feels that our actions are meaningless, that our efforts have no effect in this sea of language.
People:	Free us, God, for a struggle that rises above these words.
Leader:	Forgive us for straying and stumbling, for our weariness and our fear of hoping.
People:	Open our hearts, Holy One, so that we can embrace the LOGOS which is the word made flesh, the living power of love in our lives.
ALL:	Hear our prayer, our word, growing into flesh in this community. Amen.

73

O Spirit of Life, who touches all that we are, we know in our hearts that we deny the fullness of life which You offer us in every waking moment. We know that we are numb and tired, and that participation in evil often seems easier than resistance. Forgive us, Holy Parent. Forgive our willful ways, and the selfish wanderings of our hearts. Open our eyes to the suffering of our sisters and brothers and direct our hands in the easing of their pain. Open our ears to the cries of those who are wounded, sick, and in pain. And open our arms to receive those who need us in the embracing power of Your love. O God of justice, create in us clean hearts and renewed spirits so that we may do all this and more. This we ask so that all might have life, and have it in great abundance. Amen.

74

Creating and Healing God, we come this day as a covenant people struggling to do Your will in a world that pulls and drags on us with a weight that we sometimes find much too heavy. There are times, God, when it is easier for us not to look or feel or risk because there is so much with which we must contend. There are times, Loving Spirit, when we turn from the reality of Your presence in our lives because it frightens us. And there are times, Gentle Master, when we turn even from the painful cries of sisters and brothers because our own pain is so great. Forgive us our stumbling, wandering way, O God. Have mercy on us, and grant us the healing power to let go of our fears so that we may find true joy in the struggle to be faithful to Your way in this world. Turn our faces to each other so that we might see the light of Your love in the reality of this community. We ask this in the name of the crucified and risen Christ, Amen.

75

Gracious God, this morning as we gather in worship, it is hard to slow the pace of our lives so that we may sense Your rhythm in our hearts. The world demands so much, Master. It never tires of competing for our total attention, and it thumps out a rhythm that is very different from Yours. We know, God, that where You sing to the rhythms of all Creation, the world would have us sing its own song. We know that where You offer reconciliation and new life, the world offers brokenness and death. And God, we are so often weary and tired that it becomes an easy thing to tap our feet to sounds that are not of Your making. We confess that we have turned from Your ways and given in to the ways of the world. We acknowledge that we have not heard the cries of sisters and brothers who suffer; that we keep too much for ourselves while others must do without; that we lose sight of the power of Your compassion and forgiveness. Have mercy on us, Holy Spirit. Forgive us for our wandering ways, and give us new vision so that we may turn from the ways of this world to offer our lives as instruments for the doing of Your will. Help us, Gentle One, to know that we have been taken hold of by Christ Jesus. Grant that we may find a willingness to give up all for You and for the ministry You give us. We pray this in Jesus' name, Amen.

76

Most Loving God, we can scarcely comprehend the scope of Your forgiveness, we can hardly believe Your amazing care for us. We confess that often we close ourselves off from Your saving presence; and in our pride, we withhold forgiveness from other people. Through the power of Your Holy Spirit, grant us the assurance of Your love. May our hearts be filled with joy and thanksgiving for the grace which overflows with love toward others. Amen.

77

Holy God, whose name is Love, this day we enter together into a sanctuary of the heart. We come together as a separate, unconnected people in search of healing and wholeness. We gather quietly, looking for something resembling hope in a world filled with pain and sorrow.

But even as we gather, God, our feet are unsure of the path. We slip, often unknowing, into despair and anger, lending our energies and our hearts to destruction instead of building, pain instead of healing. Forgive us, Holy Spirit. Have mercy on us for slipping and falling; for failing to recognize the connections we have between us as Your children. Forgive us for being unable to seize the joy we have in being Your community, and empower us to begin anew. Help us, Creating Love, to let go of our fears and our inadequacies in order to embrace the power of Your way in the universe; the love of Your child, Jesus. We ask this in His name, Amen.

78

Sovereign God, we know You to be the God of endless possibilities. We know, if we choose to recall, the countless times that You have turned defeat into victory, and sorrow into joy. And we also know of the deep yearnings You have for us as Your children. But so often, Master, we are seduced and captured by a world that would place limits on You and have us serve the principalities and powers of this age. Have mercy on us, Creating God. Forgive us for the countless times we have denied the reality of new life You offer. Liberate us with Your loving grace and empower us for the ministry of justice and peace to which You call us. This we pray in hope and faith in the new life that awaits us, even now. Amen.

79

Leader: Great and Wonderful God, there are times in the lives we lead when hope evaporates.

People: There are times when the love we know You offer seems to wander off in confusion.

Right: *(indicating those sitting on the right side of the sanctuary)* There are times when the confidence we have in being Your children seems to sour and we awake to a numbing paralysis of fear and despair.

Left: *(indicate left side)* In these times, O God, it is easier to hide in the folds of a culture that would deny Your love.

Leader: It seems safer to keep silent and acquiesce to the pain and suffering around us.

Right: Forgive us, God.

Left: Have mercy on us.

ALL: Forgive our insecurity and our fears and teach us the joy of loving, not only each other, but the whole of Creation. We ask this in the name of the Child who came so that we might know the abundance of this love. Amen.

80

O God of our lives, we join together today in a knowing prayer. We know that You are present throughout the whole Creation, and wait only for us to open our hearts enough to embrace You and Your will for us. Yet, in our quiet moments, Holy One, we know, too, that Your presence is something that we would rather not know about. For in embracing You, we are aware that there is much about us, our communities, and our institutions that You would have us change. And, God, there is nothing that frightens us more than change.

Forgive us, Loving God. Free us from the fear of change, and lead us into the adventure of new life in Your Holy Spirit. Help us to know that change is part of Your plan for us and for all of Creation. We pray this in the hope that we might open our hearts and our church to the power of Your spirit in the days and years that lay ahead. Give us strength. Give us courage. Give us joy. In this hope, and before Christ and Your Holy Spirit, we offer this prayer, Amen.

81

Holy Spirit, Guide and Friend, we are here as ones not so different from that community gathered so long ago. Yet we are different in many ways. Perceptions, experiences, culture, race, gender, sexuality, and nationality stand before us as potential dividing walls. It is easy to succumb to the myth that these differences must divide us. It is easy to wall ourselves off into the limited reality of our own experiences. We know that there are times when this is true. We know that there are times when our own fear acts as a bricklayer, building walls and creating divisions.

Forgive us God. Forgive the fear that seeps into us and give us the courage to give that fear to You. Forgive our narrow focus and our ties to once and long ago. Grant us, we pray, the grace to embrace the fullness of who we are together. Give us vision and enthusiasm to claim the great strength found in our wonderful diversity. Hear our prayer, O God, and fill our hearts with the fire of Pentecost, even as we pray in the name of Your child, Jesus Christ, Amen.

82

Gentle Spirit, as Your people we move through life too often denying our frailties. We live convinced of our own strength, unwilling to see ourselves as vulnerable and dependent, not only upon each other, but upon You and Your Creating Love. Forgive us, God, for the times we walk in arrogance; for the moments we deny the truth of Your compassionate love; for the days and weeks that we make choices that hurt and cause pain to others. Remake us, Creating God. Build us again into a community that lives out the healing reality of Your presence in the world. Encircle us with loving power and dare us to discipleship. In Christ's name we pray, Amen.

83

Loving God, we come this day as a community committed to the gift of ministry You have given us. We claim the power of Your love and forgiveness, and long to move forward with one heart into the holy work of healing, love and liberation. But even as our hearts stir, O God, we feel the tugging strings of fear and doubt. Even as we plan and strategize, we sense the power of a world that will not welcome our work. We admit these fears and doubts, Holy Spirit, and open our hearts before You in prayer. Bind us up. Open our arms to the support and love we have in each other. Take away our selfish needs and wants and teach us the simple creating beauty of Your self-giving love. Diminish our egos and fill us with the wholeness that is our being in You. We ask this in hope and in joy, Amen.

84

Creating God, we hear the voice of the Spirit, calling each of us forward into lives of healing and joy. But we are reluctant, God. Like children hiding from a mother's call at dinner time, we crouch quietly in our fears trying not to hear; trying not to respond. We cling to these things which are familiar and comforting, not wishing to risk the unknown, uncontrollable power of Your love in our lives. Forgive us God. Teach us how to let go—how to risk as a servant people in Your name. Renew our vision and rebuild our strength. In the name of Jesus the Christ, we pray. Amen.

85

Great and Gracious God, we come before You this day as ones who yearn for the wonder of Your love. We join together in singing and in praise, and we seek the face of wonder and compassion in our lives. Yet in truth, Holy Spirit, our fear binds us as surely as a rope. We are afraid of pain, afraid of rejection, afraid of failure, and afraid of being afraid. Forgive us our fears, Great Healer, and grant us the power to walk away from the ropes that bind us. Have mercy on us for living in illusions and half-truths and missing the power of Your way of being. Sensitize us, open us, and fill us with Your Holy Spirit, O God, so that we might claim the joy which is in our struggle and leave our fears behind. In Christ's name we pray, Amen.

86

Leader: God who lifts us up and calls us into lives of healing, we offer this prayer to You.

People: We know, God, who we are. And we know also the pain of our participation in the suffering and oppression of our own sisters and brothers here and around the globe.

Leader: It is our own suffering.

People: It is our own oppression.

Leader: It is the continuing crucifixion of our Lord, Jesus Christ.

People: Have mercy on us, Gracious Master.

Leader: Forgive our willful blindness, and release us from the paralysis of inaction and fear.

People: Teach us to reach out with the same love You had for us when You gave us the gift of Your child, Jesus.

Leader: As we come to the cross this night, in fear and trembling, we too feel the sorrow,

People: We too feel Your love.

All: In this love and in this sorrow, renew us Holy Spirit. Make us whole in the light of Your compassion. Hear this confession, O God. For we pray in the name of Jesus the Christ, who was crucified and is crucified still; who has risen and rises still in hope and power.

87

Loving and Gracious Spirit, we are a community of frail and frightened people who need, not only the healing and liberating power of Your love in our lives, but each other as well. We need trust, affection, support and joy. We need, Spirit of Love, to know You in the faces and arms of our sisters and brothers.

But there are so many times when we feel caught—paralyzed by our fear. There are moments when, knowing the right thing to do, we automatically choose the wrong. Worse, there are moments when we stand mute and silent in the face of pain, suffering and injustice.

Forgive us, God. Have mercy on us for our inaction. Forgive our unwillingness to embrace Your love in the love of the people whom we touch every day. Teach us, Spirit, that it is in the giving of love that we find and receive love; that it is in the serving that we are served, and that it is in risking that we will find our true security. We offer this prayer in hope and in knowledge of the new life we have in Your child Jesus, Amen.

88

Gracious and Gentle God, in these days of reflection and penitence, we stop and sense the reality of Your presence among us. We pause in the silence to ponder the gift of the Child, and the suffering that was His, and must be ours if we be faithful. In the moments of our reflection, Loving Spirit, we find that fear reaches from the mist to touch and hold us. We find that the world around us speaks unceasingly to us, calling us to forget the love we have in You. It becomes easy, God of Love, to close ranks with the blind and numb and to leave the struggling community behind. We are afraid of the power of Your community; shy of the intimacy it offers, and we run, tripping over excuses all the way. Forgive us God. Have mercy on us as we try to rise and move through the paralysis of our fear. Forgive us for being unwilling to risk, unwilling to hope, unwilling to make ourselves vulnerable. Walk among us, Holy Spirit, and touch the weak and painful places. Heal us. Make us whole. For truly, we belong to You and no other. In the name of the crucified and risen Christ, we pray, Amen.

89

God of steadfast love and purpose, You know how we rush to serve You and stand by You in the glow of success and popularity. You know also that we live our lives seeking the safety of achievement and good times. Yet when the tide turns, O God, and there is suffering and oppression in our path, we turn in fear and despair, believing that we have no power to heal; no love to give. We run, hoping to shed the weight of our responsibility as people of faith, as members of the human family. Forgive us, God. Have mercy on us for our unwillingness to risk in the act of living and loving. Forgive us for our willingness to trust in most anything but the power of Your Creative Love. Teach us the joy of this day, we pray, and grant that we may stride alongside Your Child, willing and able to follow Him, wherever His love may take us. Amen.

90

God of Love, we come this day as a covenant people struggling to do Your will in a world that pulls and drags on us with a weight that we sometimes find much too heavy. There are times, God, when it is easier for us not to look or feel or risk because there is so much with which we must contend. There are times, Loving Spirit, when we turn from the reality of Your presence in our lives because it frightens us. And there are times, Gentle Master, when we turn even from the painful cries of sisters and brothers because our own pain is so great. Forgive us our stumbling, wandering way, O God. Have mercy on us, and grant us the healing power to let go of our fears so that we may find true joy in the struggle to be faithful to Your way in this world. Turn our faces to each other so that we might see the light of Your love in the reality of this community. We ask this in the name of the crucified and risen Christ, Amen.

91

O God who claims our hearts as wellsprings of love and healing, hear our prayer. We know that we gather as ones who participate in structures of sin and evil. We know that our government takes the taxes we pay and uses them for death, oppression, and suffering. We know, as we worship this day, that thousands die around the world in the name of wealth and empire, and that we are complicit. Even our church is complicit, God, and our hearts are broken. We are broken and brought low with despair over our own participation in the systems and structures of death. Have mercy on us. Have mercy on us, Loving Spirit. Forgive us for being timid, afraid, unwilling to stand in faith for the peace and justice which we know are the expressions of Your love for the whole of Creation. Breathe your breath upon us, God, and fill us with the Power of Your Spirit. Teach us the joy of risky discipleship, the wonder of our voices and our lives as they speak in Christlike harmony, saying "NO" to death and suffering and "YES" to life and healing. Join our hands and hearts and make us new. We pray this in the name of Your child Jesus, who comes now and always among us, Amen.

92

Sovereign God, we know You to be the God of endless possibilities. We know, if we choose to recall, the countless times that You have turned defeat into victory, and sorrow into joy. And we know too of the deep yearnings You have for us as Your children. But so often, Master, we are seduced and captured by a world that places limits on You and has us serve the principalities and powers of this age. Have mercy on us, Creating God. Forgive us for the countless times we have denied the reality of new life You offer. Liberate us with Your loving grace and empower us for the ministry of justice and peace to which You call us. This we pray in hope and faith in the new life that awaits us, even now. Amen.

93

O God whose name is Love, we stand in the midst of a world who would give You other names; a world who would name You "violence," "national pride," and "money." It's a world, O God, whose power is strong, and it is true that we have slid into its grip. We have participated in the death-dealing reality of this world with our acquiescence and our silence. Have mercy on us, Gracious One. Forgive us for giving in to the temptations of material things and blinding our eyes in fear and confusion. Teach us the deep power of the love which You would have us claim as Yourself. Help us to know it and to accept it into our hearts so that we may stand as one in truth and spirit. We pray this in the hope that life will triumph over death and in the name of Your Child, who showed us how possible this triumph is. Amen.

94

Leader: The Voice of the Holy echoes throughout our lives.
People: We stumble about, unhearing and uncertain.
Leader: Love of the Holy embraces us as a mother caring for a child.
People: Yet we deny that love, choosing fear and anger instead.
Leader: The Justice of the Holy rises up before us in the faces of the suffering and oppressed.
People: Yet we walk on by, blinded by a world of things and acquisitions.
Leader: The Peace of the Holy knocks impatiently at the door of our heart.
People: And we pretend that no one is home.
ALL: Forgive us, Holy One. Have mercy on us for our unwillingness to accept You into our lives. Forgive us for not hearing the call of Your Way in the world. Awaken our spirits, O God, and renew our hearts for the receiving of Your gift of ministry. This is our prayer to You and our hope for us. Amen.

95

Great and Wonderful God, the power of new life flows in us this day as we come to celebrate and sing. It is a power that moves and grows throughout our lives, Gracious One, but so often it is a power that we deny and refuse to embrace. The new life that You offer calls us to change, and we are afraid. The new life that You offer calls us to risk and we are terrified. The new life You offer calls us to die so that we may live again, and we turn away in numbness and confusion. Forgive us God. Have mercy on us for our fear and confusion. Forgive our halting, uncertain commitment, and our unwillingness to hope. Create in us, God, the will to love and to heal. Renew us for lives of joy, and walk with us as we move forward together in the new life You offer even now. In the name of the Risen Christ we pray, Amen.

96

Leader: O God who walks among us, we know that we have deluded ourselves, believing and living as though we can make it on our own.
People: We admit it. We confess our denial of the killing realities in which we live.
Leader: When we stop to pay attention, we can feel ourselves, slipping, stumbling, and falling from the wonder of Your Creating Love to the depths of our own anger and willfulness.
People: Lift us up, Strong and Gentle One. Forgive us. Take away our

delusions and our false assumptions of strength. Teach us the true strength and power of love and compassion, and lead us on the path of Your justice and Your peace.

ALL: We pray this in the name of the one whose blood was shed so that we might all find forgiveness. Amen.

(adapted from the writings of St. Gregory of Nazianzus)

97

Like Jacob, waking from the dream, we come suddenly to know that You are in this place. Yet we stand in awe and wonder, reaching out for You, clutching only at empty air. It's true, God, that You are here. We can feel Your presence in the touch and affection of this community. But we forget, Loving Spirit, that Your presence among us is not something to be grasped or possessed. We do not see that You are a reality to belived and embraced as we climb the stairs on our journey. Forgive us God for trying to catch You and label You. Have mercy on us for limiting the power of Your Creating Love with definitions and theories, and grant us free and open hearts for the living out of Your presence in our lives. We pray this now in the hope and promise of new life. Amen.

98

Great and Gentle God, our prayer this day is the echo of Peter's voice. With him, we claim, in our baptism, and in our words that You are the Messiah, that You have come among us to give us a new way of being: a new reality in God's love. This new and different way feels so right, God. It feels right to let go of anger and embrace love. It feels right to halt our participation in pain and death. And it feels right to forgive even as we receive Your forgiveness. But in truth, Holy One, we live in a world that challenges the way we choose each step of our journey. We are part of a world that would dilute and dissolve us, a world that mocks and ridicules our choice of faith. And sometimes, O God, it is just too difficult. Forgive us when we shy away in the face of so powerful an opposition. Have mercy on us when we lose our clarity and our vision in the face of this violent world. Hold us close, loving Savior, and help us to feel Your constant presence in our lives. Restore our vision, sharpen our clarity so that we might claim a ministry in the warmth of Your love. Hear our prayer, Gracious One, in the name of Your child Jesus, Amen.

99

Gracious Spirit, too often our lives are caught in the frenzied grip of a world that would have us turn from love; a world that would blind and numb us to the truth of our connectedness. In this moment, Holy God, we remember too well the many times when we have found ourselves isolated and alone. We recall that courage, hope and power dwell, not only within each human heart, but in the common heart of the community as well. Forgive us for surrendering to the pain of this world. Have mercy on us for the many ways we find to numb ourselves into isolation. Be with us, God. Teach us to find within each heart the will to be vulnerable; the hope which can heal. We ask this in the name of the one who came that we might know love; that we might become love, Amen.

100

Loving Master, we rise in hope this day as ones who claim a vision of our earth as home; a vision of ourselves as partners in your ongoing act of Creation. But we rise, God, also in shame and guilt as we comprehend the reality of our participation in the destruction of Your world. Forgive us, we plead, for lifestyles of arrogance and greed which pollute and poison this beautiful planet. Have mercy on us for our shortsighted selfishness and our unwillingness to see ourselves as one within this sphere of life. Renew us, we pray. Create in us clean hearts and new spirits for the healing of the world we have helped to wound so deeply. We offer this prayer to You as sign and symbol of a transformation that will not stop at the doorway of this church. Amen.

101

Leader: God be with you.
People: And also with you.
ALL: As God is with us, so we lift up our hearts in prayer.
Leader: Sovereign God, we would stop now and shake free the quiet brokenness which grasps our hearts in numbing paralysis.
People: But deep down, we feel that paralysis is better than pain.
Leader: Deep down, the numbness somehow seems better than the experiences of our hearts, our feelings about life and pain.
People: Deep down, we are afraid to feel, not only pain, but joy, love and anger as well.
Leader: Forgive us God.
People: Have mercy on us for being swept up in this tide of numbness.
Leader: Revive us again and awaken our hearts.
ALL: Lift us up and make us new, Loving Spirit. Teach us to risk the joy of being alive in You. Help us to grasp the power of Your healing love and to move with it into a world that is broken and ill. We ask this in the hope of our own healing and in the knowledge of Your unending love for us. Amen.

102

Great and Wondrous God, in this moment, we pause in apprehension to open our hearts before You. We long for the child's vision of hope, the joyous laughter and smiles untouched by fear or pain. There are moments, Holy God, when this longing is more than we can stand. Forgive us for having shed our child-hearts. Have mercy on us for leaving the openness of love behind in the name of protection and security. Grant that we might reach out together in newness of life, and help us to know that we may once again be truly Your children if only we would risk it. In the name of the one who risked all that we might have this chance, we pray. Amen.

PRAYERS FOR THE STATE OF GOD'S CHURCH

The Church is a wonderfully confused blur of tradition, institution, and community. It is often difficult to sort it all out while maintaining a clarity of vision and call, of mission and hope. And so, in faith, the community prays for the state of God's Church.

103

Strong and Gentle God, we are a people who know in our hearts the kind of strength You would have us embrace. We know of a strength found in vulnerability and openness. We understand the healing power of love and forgiveness. We ask, Holy Spirit, that this understanding and knowledge be born into the life of Your Church. May we be as midwives at the birth of a new vision for the Church. And may it be a vision of peace and justice as the core of Your Gospel, rather than of membership numbers and dollar signs. May it be a vision of faithfulness rather than effectiveness. And may the reality of Your presence guide this vision now and always as we move forward in Christ's name. Amen.

104

God of our lives, we gather here as ones called out in faith to be Your hands and Your voice in the world. We come, longing to witness to the reality of Your love in the midst of days where vision is dim and joy hides beneath veils of sorrow. Grant us strength and courage to be the Church, O God. Lift us up and guide us as we claim the power of Your love over violence and oppression. And hold us close, Loving Master, as we claim also the joy we have in You and in this community. In Christ's name we pray, Amen.

105

Loving God, this prayer is not for the sake of some institution or doctrine. This prayer is for the hope which we name as Your Church. The Church which stands on hope and claims the healing message of Your child Jesus, is a Church which understands itself as a site for struggle; a Church which envisions itself as an agent for change; a Church which embraces all people as sisters and brothers and builds its sanctuaries out of selfless love and forgiveness. For this Church, O God, and for those who would lift it up and participate in it, we pray. Give strength, send joy, and soothe the worried brows. In the name of the child Jesus we pray, Amen.

106

O God, this day we pray that Your vision of wholeness for Creation will reach into the heart of everyone who claims the name of Christ. Touch our eyes with this vision, Lord, so that we may press on as a great cloud of witnesses, placing our lives in Your hands as the means to a loving and reconciled world. We pray this, knowing the risks and embracing the hope of new life in the resurrection. Amen.

107

Loving God, this morning we come together as Your children to celebrate the entrance into the city. We come as Your community, Your church, hoping to catch a glimpse of the One who comes in Your name. Yet, even as we try to peer over the crowd, we sense that this "One" is in our midst already. We know, down deep, that even as we cheer, the call comes to us to go forward in the name of God. Grant, Gracious One, as the dust settles and the palm leaves lay quiet in the road, that we take up the call and bear witness to Your healing and liberation. We pray this in the hope and power of the resurrection, Amen.

108

Gracious God who brings forth water from stone, our prayer this day is a resurrection prayer; a cry for new life. It is a prayer for a church which sleeps soundly through the cries of the hungry and the roar of the guns. A hope for a church caught too often in the web of structure and polity; a plea for a church too busy counting heads to speak the truth. It is a prayer for us, Living Spirit. For it is our church: our hope and our plea. Renew Your church, Loving Parent, and through us, call it to faithfulness and wholeness as we strive to be faithful doers of Your will in our lives. In the name of Christ, we offer this prayer. Amen.

109

Holy and Wondrous God, this day we gather as Your church to claim the love You hold out for us without condition. We know, Gracious One, that we are accepted just as we are—broken, hurting, angry, and oh, so tired. The love You embody is so total that we often fail to embrace it in our lives. The love You express is so powerful that we back away and miss bringing it into the life of our church. We pray in this hour that we will have the courage to strive, to laugh, and to give all so that Your church may grow beyond the bounds of institution and doctrine to the same active and creating love that You have given us in the child Jesus. Be with us, make us aware of You in all things, and above all, Sovereign One, help us to sing the new song. Amen.

110

God of our lives, we gather here as ones called out in faith, to be Your hands and Your voice in the world. We come, longing to witness to the reality of Your Love in the midst of days where vision is dim and joy hides beneath veils of sorrow. Grant us strength and courage to be the church, O God. Lift us up and guide us as we claim the power of Your love over violence and oppression, the wonder of Your spirit over numbness and decay. Hold us close, Loving Master, as we claim also the joy we have in You and in this community. In Christ's name we pray, Amen.

111

Loving and Gracious God, on this day of rising, we gather as the body of Christ, knowing that too often our church lives as though the stone was never rolled aside; as though there were no empty tomb. We know of the practicalities and politics which draw Your church into the morass of compromise and sin, O God. We know of a church that is complicit with the principalities and power of this age; a church which hesitates to pick up the cross and walk toward resurrection. But we know, too, of a church in struggle. We know of a church which claims an ancient and wonderful vision of healing and liberation. Loving God, we ask for strength and courage to be that church. We pray for vision and for the joy which comes to us as we gaze into the tomb today. Most gracious God, we pray for the courage and conviction to be Your loving community in this time and place. In the name of the Risen Christ, Amen.

112

Great and Gentle God, as we gather this day to open our hearts to the power of Your love, rest a patient hand on our shoulder and turn us to the healing of Your church. Open our ears so that we can hear Your call to a new way of being. Open our hearts to the joy of the good community, and free our hands for the lifelong struggle for faithfulness. We pray this in the hope and certainty of new life in Your child, Jesus. Amen.

113

O Great and Wonderful God, Your church stands in these days on the edge of renewal. Leaning and weaving, it travels in a world which resists the compassionate power of Your Spirit. It is layered and etched with centuries of struggle and stumbling, and needs the healing touch of new life. On this day, Creating Friend, as we look toward the coming of the Spirit on Pentecost, we ask for the patience, love, and humor we need to empower our church for change and for struggle. Be our counsel and our guide as we move together to claim our heritage as the ones who bear the name of Your child, Jesus, the Christ. Amen.

114

Creating Spirit, this morning finds Your church gathered in hope to receive the Spirit. As a Pentecostal people, we lift our voices in thanksgiving as the Body of Christ grows in strength and wisdom. Be with us as we stand together to face the wind of Your love, and hold us in Your arms as Your children in this world so that we might become more bold, take more risks, and stand as ones authentically struggling to be faithful. In Christ's name we pray, Amen.

115

Gracious and Giving God, as we come this day into each other's warmth, we pray for the strength and power to weave a new vision for Your Church. Too often, we walk as the disciples walked, unseeing and unknowing in the presence of the Christ. Too often, practicality and expedience are more important than faithfulness. Grant, Holy One, that as Your children we may claim this vision and make it our own as we participate fully in the liberating reality of the Kingdom that Jesus came to proclaim. For it is in His name that we pray, Amen.

116

O God who calls us into community so that we may receive the gift of ministry, hear our prayer. We sit tonight on the margins of a church bound up in the ways of the world. It is a church weighted down and constrained by its attachments to social categories and divisions which wound our people, and even the whole of Creation. On this night we gather to proclaim a different kind of church. We come to lift up a community of a people of faith who break down the dividing walls between us and struggle to live out the truth that we are one. No longer is there black or white, male or female, gay or straight. No longer will the judgments and labels of a broken world turn us from each other. Empower us, Holy Spirit. Create in us the courage and the joy we need to be Your church. Move among us and bring us together in the common vision of justice, peace and liberation for all. We pray this in the certainty of new life in our midst. Amen.

117

O Loving and Tender God, this intstitution that we call Your church, like all our institutions, is not pefect. Yet we struggle to center our efforts in your Gospel and in the example of your child Jesus. We pray, O Master, for strength and courage to be Your church; to be a beacon of hope and healing for the world, and a center where justice and peace find a home in our hearts. This we pray in joy and love, Amen.

OCCASIONAL PRAYERS

The group of newly baptized folks were sitting around having tea, and one asked, "What should we pray for today?" Everyone laughed and said all at once, "Patience!" It's true, in any church community, patience is a necessary ingredient. But there are also prayers for many things, for many moments and occasions. These are but a few.

118

A PRAYER FOR AWARENESS (UNISON): Gracious God, awaken in us a love of Creation. Renew in us a Spirit that yearns for justice, and make us open to the power of the peace which You offer. For we know, even as we sit this morning in prayer, that what You promise is a new reality, a new way of being, a realm of healing and wholeness which lives and breathes in and around us. Touch us, God. Shake the sleep of numbness from our eyes and bring us to faithful lives of justice, peace, and wholeness. Amen.

119

PRAYER POR AWARENESS:

Leader: O God, we are persons, each of us.

People: We stand alone in history, yet there are others, only a hand's length away, with whom we could join our spirits, to bring into our being a soul-force that might transform the world.

Leader: Make us aware, O God, of the pain of the world.

People: Help us to hear the cries of the oppressed,

Leader: The poor,

People: The prisoners.

Leader: Make us aware, O God, of the joys of life.

People: Help us to hear the beauty of the earth,

Leader: Of people,

People: Of ourselves and of the whole of Creation.
Leader: O God, help us to listen.
People: For in listening, we will speak our love,
Leader: And by listening
People: We will be moved to act in faith.
ALL: Amen.

120

A RESURRECTION PRAYER: Gracious and Loving God, it's Easter morning. Everywhere we turn there is evidence of the Resurrection. As we open our eyes, we see the whole Creation bursting with new life. As we open our hearts, we feel a surge of healing and new life that enters into our relationships with families, partners, and loved ones. And as we open our arms, we feel the overwhelming power of the connections between us all. Grant, God of Life, that we as Your people may learn to embrace the resurrection of Your child, Jesus, as a reality that never ends; as a life that we may choose and choose again. We pray this now and always in Jesus' name, Amen.

121

A LITANY OF HOPE:

Leader: God swore to David a sure oath, and will not turn back from it.
People: "One from the fruit of your body I will set on your throne.
Leader: If your children keep my covenant and my testimonies which I shall teach them.
People: Their children shall also forever sit upon your throne."
Leader: For God has chosen Zion.
People: And has desired it for a habitation:
Leader: This is my resting place forever;
People: Here I dwell, for I have desired it.
Leader: I will abundantly bless its provisions;
People: I will satisfy its poor with bread.
Leader: Its priests I will clothe with salvation,
People: And its saints will shout for joy. Amen. (Psalm 132: 11-16)

122

A PRAYER FOR ILLUMINATION: Gracious and Loving God, may the words of the scriptures find us with hearts and arms outstretched with a yearning and quiet joy. For Your word is precious to us as we struggle in Your name to be a faithful people. Amen.

123

A HOPING PRAYER: God of grace and wisdom, our prayer this day falls like petals from summer flowers. The scent of their leaving promises seeds and new beginnings to come. Yet often, we look beyond the simple images and realities You provide. We demand proof and substance, refusing to hope while hope itself grows before our very eyes. Sustain us, God. Pull our hearts together as we reach for this promise of new life. Clothe us with the love of Your child Jesus, who came among us so that we might all look to see flowers, seeds, and the promise of new life and wholeness. Amen.

124

A HOPING PRAYER: O God, hear us as our hands reach out—each for the other. Love us as we struggle to be faithful doers of Your will. Know, Loving Spirit, that we will not be lax in celebrating. We will not be lazy as we join in the festival of servanthood. We will risk enthusiasm, we will risk hope. We are ablaze with the power of Your Love, Creating One, and yearn to be a living, burning offering to the way of being that You have offered us and offer us still. In Christ's name we pray, Amen.

125

A PRAYER OF UNITY: Holy God, You have called us together as one people, and in Your love You have shown us the way to participate in the reality of a healing and whole community. Lead us, Spirit of Love. Empower us so that we might grow together in deed and in truth. Help us to know the depth of love and compassion which is the substance of Your being in us and in the whole of Creation. In the name of the Child, we pray, Amen.

126

A PRAYER OF AWARENESS: God of our lives, we know that You are the foundation of all that is. You provide with such abundance that nothing is lacking for full and whole lives, not just for humanity, but for the whole of Your Creation. We pray in this hour that we, as humans, will take our place as partners and healers, becoming one with You and with our earth. We pray this in the name of the One who came among us that the whole of Creation may be renewed, Amen.

127

PRAYER OF HOPE: O God whose shadow stretches o'er us like the cooling branches of a summer tree, gather us now as children who seek new answers. Lift us up in hope and power, and let our very lives be the voice of Your yearning for justice and Your will for peace. In the name of Christ, we pray, Amen.

128

A LITANY OF RECONCILIATION:

Leader: We are a people broken and separated.
People: We long for healing.
Leader: Our lives are poor because we do not have the richness of each other's experiences to nourish us.
People: But that which is broken can be healed,
Leader: And that which has been separated can be united.
ALL: Reconcile us God. Bring about the change which comes from Your healing love. Transform us. Mold us. Make us new in the Spirit of unity, acceptance and love. Amen.

129

THE PRAYER OF UNITY: Great and Wonderful God, as we have shared this bread and this cup, so may we share together the warmth and intimacy of the love You have to offer through Your child, Jesus. Amen.

130

A HOPING PRAYER: Loving Spirit, fill me now with the power of Your hoping. Wrap the gentle movement of Your presence around my moments and my days, and teach me the fullness of Your justice. Amen.

131

A LENTEN LITANY:

Leader: Gracious God, grant that we may not be conformed to "this world," but that we might love it and serve it.
People: Grant that we may never shrink from being instruments of Your peace because of the criticism we will receive.
Leader: Grant that we may love You without fear of "this world."

People: Grant that we may never confuse the wonder of Your power from any other power on this earth.

Leader: May we love You, Holy One, and our neighbors as ourselves.

People: May we remember the wounded, the poor and the prisoner, the sick and the lonely, the young searchers, the tramps, the homeless, the lost, and the lonely.

ALL: May we embrace these all, and remember them not just in spirit, but in the truth of the Christ who is in them, in us, and in all things. Amen.

(adapted from Alan Paton)

132

PRAYER OF HOPE: Loving Friend, we walk so often in shadows which darken and obscure our way that we forget the shape and texture of hope. We are told that it is empty wishing. We are asked to be still and "hope" for better tomorrows. But God, we know that the ground of our hope is You, and that our hope is born as we embrace the struggle to be a faithful people who live out Your vision of justice and liberation. Grant us strength, and grant us vision, Holy Spirit, so that our hope may be the music of souls united in the healing and liberating work of Your Son Jesus. For it is in His name that we pray, Amen.

133

A COVENANT PRAYER: Gracious and Wondrous God, we are a people of faith who are awash in the wonderful power of Your love. Everywhere we turn, Your forgiveness reaches out to touch our hearts. We know in the healing You have brought us that we are chosen for ministry, selected to be the bringers of justice, and builders of a new community. Holy One, in this hour we choose our choseness and accept our call. With the oneness we have in Christ, we reach to meet You in the living of our lives. Give us hope, fill us with joy and move us to boldness in the ministry of Your church. Amen.

THE LORD'S PRAYER

There is perhaps no more powerful prayer within our tradition than "The Lord's Prayer." Trying to get hold of its essence, its power and the depth of meaning can be helped by trying different versions of the prayer.

Over the years at Washington Square UMC, we have tried slightly different variations, changing shading and tone of the prayer to bring out different elements of its meaning.

O God, our beloved parent,
May we hold Your name as Holy in the living of our lives;
May your dominion become a reality in this community of faith.
Provide us we pray, with enough,
And forgive us our debts, our sins and our stumbling,
For we will also forgive each one who is in debt to us.
And do not put us to the test, but set us free from all evil.
For it is Your power we claim above all else, now and forevermore. Amen.

†

Our God, who is our Creator and Redeemer,
Holy is Your name.
May we build Your reality here in this place.
Provide us, we pray, with enough to meet our needs.
And forgive us our debts, our sins, and our stumbling, as we will also forgive.
Help us to avoid the temptations of this world,
And save us from our participation in evil.
For it is Your power we acknowledge, now and always, Amen.

†

O God, our beloved Parent,
May we hold Your name as holy in the living of our lives;
May Your dominion become a reality in this community of faith.
Provide us, we pray, with enough.
And forgive us our debts and our stumbling,
For we will also forgive each one who is in debt to us.

And do not put us to the test. But set us free from all evil.
For Yours is the dominion, the power and the glory forever. Amen.

†

Gracious God of love and power,
We claim Your name as Holy.
May the reality of Your way of being live in us and in this community of faith.
Provide us, we pray, with enough to meet our needs.
And forgive us our debts as we forgive our debtors.
Save us God, from times of trial, and deliver us from our participation in evil.
For it is Your power we acknowledge in the world, both now and forever. Amen.

†

O God, our Creator and Redeemer,
Holy is Your name.
May we claim Your way of being in the world,
And risk doing Your will in all things.
Provide us, we pray, with enough to meet our needs
And give us strength to resist a world of greed and harmful power.
Forgive us our sins and our stumbling
For we will forgive others who have sinned against us and caused us pain.
And do not put us to the test, Holy One, but set us free from all evil.
For it is Your power we acknowledge in the world, and no other. Amen.

†

Our God, who is our Creator and Redeemer,
Holy is Your name.
Empower us in building a community devoted to Your way of being,
Which is the way of life, hope, and wholeness.
Provide us, we pray, with enough to meet our needs,
And forgive us our debts, our sins, and our stumbling,
For we will forgive in like manner.
Help us to avoid the temptations of our social world,
And save us from our participation in evil.
For it is Your power we acknowledge, now and always, Amen.

†

Our God, who is in heaven, Holy be Your name. Your Kingdom come, Your will be done on earth as it is in heaven. Give us this day our daily bread. Forgive us our debts as we forgive those who are indebted to us. Save us from the temptations of this world, and deliver us from evil. For Yours is the Kingdom, Yours is the Power, and Yours is the Glory, now and forever. Amen.

Harkness '94

EUCHARISTIC PRAYERS

Our traditional rituals are important. Recasting prayers, rituals and rites into the language understood by the community helps to give power and meaning to things that can be lost, simply because people find it hard to relate some language to their experience and context. What follows is a sampling of our efforts, to offer new versions of our beautiful traditions.

A PRAYER OF GREAT THANKSGIVING: Strong and Wonderful God, who gives us the gift of community, we rejoice this morning in the singing of a new song. Together, we lift up our whole community as a living offering to Your Way of Being in the world. Together, we humbly claim the joy of being ones who bear the name of Your child, Jesus. This is a moment of celebration and a moment of remembering. We celebrate this family of faith, and as this community of the body of Christ grows in love and in ministry, we cannot help but remember that Jesus' body was broken for us; that his blood was spilled so that we might be free to claim the power of forgiveness and love as the way of the Realm of God.

We remember, and we know that the body of Christ is broken still wherever people struggle to be faithful. We remember, and we know that the blood of Christ is spilled where faithful people risk discipleship.

And remembering this, O God, we recall the meal. Among us we share a thousand visions of tables and loving friends: scenes of laughter, and scenes of betrayal. We also share a vision which we hold in common, Loving God. And as we share the bread and the cup today, we lift up this vision of healing and hope; this vision of justice and peace; this vision of a Church renewed and reclaimed. It is a vision of the Body of Christ, faithful and whole. Be with us, Holy One, and send Your spirit upon this meal as we prepare to move forward together in joy and in struggle. In the name of Jesus Christ we offer this prayer. Amen.

A EUCHARISTIC PRAYER

THE INVITATION:

THE LEADER: Before us is the meal. As a people of faith, we approach this table with humility and joy. Ours is a community who claims Jesus Christ as the source of power in our lives; and it is in His name that we strike down the barriers between us and invite all who come in love to approach the table as sisters and brothers.

THE PRAYER OF GREAT THANKSGIVING:

THE LEADER: Sisters and brothers, the Living God is with us!

THE PEOPLE: We lift up our hearts to the Creating Spirit!

THE LEADER: As a people of compassion, let us give thanks and praise to the Nurturing Love in our midst:

THE PEOPLE: As a people of struggle, we raise our voices to join the chorus of the ages in singing endless praise with the very fabric of our lives.

THE LEADER: HOLY, HOLY, HOLY GOD! God who transforms power and might! Blessed are You and blessed are those who come in Your name. You are the Creative One who weaves the universe and all that is in it. Beneath our feet, You have provided the rich and wonderful tapestry of Creation, and charged us with its nurture and care. You brought all creatures into being, and linked us with them as part of Your wondrous plan for life ongoing.

THE PEOPLE: Throughout the hours and days of our being, we experience You in every moment, every thought and every feeling that washes over us in our human ways of knowing.

THE LEADER: Your power comes to us as the sun rises to warm us and light our way. Your laughter sings 'round us in busy streets and late night sidewalks. Your unending love reaches out again and again in the screech of newborn children and in the wealth of trust and love we have in each other.

THE PEOPLE: And in all this, Your love is so great, Oh God, that You gave still more. In the fullness of Your time, You sent Your only child, Jesus to walk among us as the embodiment of Your way of being, the voice of Your yearning for us.

THE LEADER: In our midst, Jesus came sauntering as one who knew joy. He laughed, ate, and drank, seeking the company of outcasts and untouchables. He proclaimed the reality of Your power, and in Your name, he healed the sick, fed the hungry, and confronted human structures which oppress and diminish Your great gift of life.

THE PEOPLE: Jesus showed us with His life that the struggle for justice, peace and liberation is a joyous Holy task; a way of being.

THE LEADER: And it was for this that we resented and feared him. Our fear hardened our hearts, and in our fear we stood by while He was handed over to be judged, tortured and executed for the high crimes of love, healing and liberation.

THE PEOPLE: On the night of his arrest, Jesus sat down once again to laugh and eat and drink. Before the meal He took a loaf of bread from the table and blessed it. Jesus broke the bread and passed it around, saying, "Take this and eat it. This is My body which will be broken for you. When you eat it, remember Me."

THE LEADER: And then He took the cup and gave thanks to you, saying, "Drink from this, all of you. It is my blood, poured out for all people so that sins may be forgiven. As often as you do this, do it in remembrance of me."

THE PEOPLE: And here we are today, Loving God, living echoes of those who sat around that long ago table with Your child.

THE LEADER: We remember our brother Jesus, and our grief overpowers us. Deep in our hearts we know that each day Jesus is betrayed, and executed. It is true that the pain and suffering of people everywhere is the pain and suffering of Jesus, our Christ. And truly, we remember.

THE PEOPLE: As we share this meal, our memory finds voice, and we declare that the love You brought to us in Jesus is a love which heals us all. Black or white, gay or straight, slave or free, the love of Jesus Christ binds us together as one with You, Oh God.

THE LEADER: It is our prayer that You will send Your blessing on us and on this meal as we celebrate the mystery of our faith and the great joy we have in Your presence among us.

ALL: This is our prayer of Thanksgiving, our cry of grief, and our tears of joy. Amen.

HYMNS FOR A NEW CHURCH

There is an old hymn which says that "time makes ancient good uncouth." This is true in a wide range of human experience, including our hymnody. These wonderful old tunes found new voice in the worship life of Washington Square UMC, trying to express the spirit of the hymn in language which would speak to a contemporary congregation.

ONWARD CHRISTIAN PACIFISTS

(A hymn for the new Church)

Music by Arthur Sullivan, 1871
Words by Schuyler Rhodes, 1990
Sung to the tune of "Onward Christian Soldiers"

Onward Christian Pacifists, walking arm in arm,
with the cross of Jesus, doing no one harm!
Christ, our gentle master, going on before,
forward in the struggle brings joy evermore!

(refrain)
Onward Christian Pacifists, walking arm in arm,
with the cross of Jesus, doing no one harm.

Love and Solidarity Satan can't abide
Sisters, brothers loving! Nothing more to hide!
Justice is our sister, peace our brother dear,
Liberation, healing, making God' s love clear!

(refrain)

On the Sabbath Holy Day, scriptures He did read,
Good news preached unto the poor, prisoners shall be freed!
Oh the blind shall see again! Dungeon doors swing wide!
We are all anointed, the Spirit is our guide!

(refrain)

A WARM, SAFE HARBOR IS OUR GOD

Words by Schuyler Rhodes, 1994
Music by Martin Luther, 1529
Sung to the tune of "A Mighty Fortress Is Our God"

A warm safe harbor is our God, a shelter never failing.
Our helper God stands with us now, a friend in spite of failings.
God loves with open heart, and always takes our part,
Our God whose name is love, comes to us as a dove
And calls us to receive our love.

Do we always strive to find, a way of our own choosing.
God calls us to turn from our own pride, and find new life in loosing.
And whose voice do we hear? Christ Jesus, he is near!
He sets the world awry and loves both you and I,
His love is without limit.

And if we struggle now for peace, and work for justice doing.
God's love will live through us today, and echo in our doing.
Our prayer and work are one. In Christ our Lord it's done!
We live our love today, and preach just what we say,
in God we have our victory! Amen!

THE REVIVAL HYMN FOR THE UNITED METHODIST CHURCH

Music: USA Campmeeting tune, 19th century
Words by Schuyler Rhodes, 1994
Sung to the tune of the "Battle Hymn of the Republic"

My eyes have seen the glory of the presence of our God,
The Holy Spirit flows unending till our hearts be thawed.
It is time to heal the hurt we've caused,
It's time to claim our hearts
For there we will find God!

Glory Glory Hallelujah
Glory Glory Hallelujah
Glory Glory Hallelujah,
God's love will heal us all.

John Wesley held his hands up high and called upon the folks
In one hand he held piety, the other justice true.
He bid us blend them both in one, a sacred balance new,
In love our church was born!

Chorus

John's brother, Charles, wrote the hymns "A Thousand Toungues" and more
Together they did preach and sing from shore to shining shore
At the coal mines and the prisons, in the factories and the streets,
In love our church was born!

Chorus

And now we've come to times of trial testing faith and more.
Our hearts are stretched by left and right, and fighting at the door.
Our proud connection feels the pain of ideology
That tears at the bond of love.

Chorus

In Christ we've come to serve the world, in Christ we live and die.
The empty tomb before us bids us give a hopeful cry,
In spite of fightings inside and our struggles all about
Our church will be reborn.

Chorus

TAKE UP THE CROSS

Music by Sydney Hugo Nicholson, 1916
Words by Schuyler Rhodes, 1994
Sung to the tune of "Lift High the Cross"

Take up the cross,
The cross of Christ take up,
And live a life
Of love and holiness!

Live, Christian, live in humble joy and love,
Forgiving all as God's forgiven you!

Take up the cross,
The cross of Christ take up
And follow love
From here to Calvary!

Let each one's life in God's own grace proclaim
We're free to love in limitless acclaim!

Take up the cross,
The cross of Christ take up,
And follow Christ
To love's redeeming Sun!

We are a people, marked before our birth,
For God's great joy in healing all the earth!

Take up the cross,
The cross of Christ take up
Till all the world knows God
Through your own life!

LET US RECLAIM OUR CHURCH

Music by Felice deGiardini, 1769
Words by Schuyler Rhodes, 1994
Sung to the tune of "Come Thou Almighty King"

Let us reclaim our church,
From this world's earthly perch.
We will not fight,
Or join the left or right,
Or judge or speak in spite,
Let's find our hearts in God
And trust in grace.

Let us choose life from above,
Embracing all people's love,
Make our arms wide,
Welcoming every heart,
Hoping they'll play a part,
And build the living art,
Of God's own heart.

The Church is God's own voice,
Echoing love's own choice,
But how we fail,
And give the Church away
To social climbing's way,
May we repent and say,
Faithful we stay!

Jesus our Christ is Lord!
Our loyalty in accord
With God's own way,
Not choosing death's dark sway
But living life each day
In love and harmony
With peace and joy.

GOD'S COUNTRY IS FOR ME

Music: Thesaurus Musicus, 1744
Words by Schuyler Rhodes, 1994
Sung to the tune of "My Country Tis of Thee"

God's country is for me,
Salvation's sweetness be,
In this I live.
To struggle faithfully,
With only thoughts of thee,
To give myself in love
To God's own dove.

Some sing for native land,
Some stand for race or clan,
I stand for God.
Some march to battlefields,
Some choose to weapons wield,
Some claim the power
Of might and sword,
I claim my Lord!

God's name is Agape
It fills my every day
With hope and joy.
Our lives with glory filled
Our struggles all fulfilled
In love and love alone
We find our home.

SIT DOWN SIT DOWN FOR JESUS

(A Protest Hymn)

Music by George Webb, 1830
Words by Schuyler Rhodes, 1994
Sung to the tune "Stand Up, Stand Up for Jesus"

Sit down, sit down for Jesus
Resisters for the cross,
Lift high your voice in protest,
Your songs will not be lost.
From air base to defense plant,
to factories built with greed,
Our hearts in love will sing out
that Christ is Lord indeed!

Link arms, link arms for Jesus,
The Spirit calls to you,
Wherever hate runs rampant,
Tis ours to dare and do.
We think not of our victory,
of stunning battles won,
We pray and live in faithfulness
and walk into God's sun.

We long to lose for Jesus,
The world's strength is weak,
When foolish Christians struggle,
We hear the powers weep.
In courtrooms and in jail cells
all Christians stand as one.
Like Paul who went before us,
We know our battle's won!

CALL US TOGETHER

(A hymn for healing)

Music by Henri F. Hemy, 1874
Words by Schuyler Rhodes, 1994
Sung to the tune of "Faith of our Fathers"

Once we were people proud and upright,
Churches were filled and convinced they were right,
Now we are plagued with doubt and with tears
Sold to a culture plagued with fear.

Call us together, call us in faith.
God of the ages, call us today.

Where there's no vision people will die,
So says the scripture and so say I.
While our Church quarrels left and right
We watch and pray, and hope for the light.

Call us together, call us in faith.
God of the ages, call us today.

We are all tempted by power and greed,
By this world, by flags unfurled,
But if we listen we hear our God call
Urging us on to reconcile all.

Call us together, call us in faith.
God of the ages, call us today.

RITES OF THE CHURCH

A RITE FOR ADMITTING NEW MEMBERS INTO THE FAITH COMMUNITY

COMMENDATION AND WELCOME:

PASTOR: As we gather here in worship and praise, we know in our hearts that the Church is more than brick and mortar; more than institution and doctrine. We know from Holy Scripture, from reason, from ancient tradition, and from our own experience that the Church of God is the community of faith bound together in struggle, love and joy; in the power of the Holy Spirit.

Today we celebrate the wonder and hope of this community as we welcome these new members into our midst.

Before us this morning are: *(Pastor gives the names of those to join the congregation)*.

They come, with open hearts, to enter formally into this community of faith. Their love of God in Christ Jesus, and their commitment to the welfare of this Christian community is evident in their active witness among us. I commend to your love and care these people whom we recognize on this day as members of our household of faith.

THE CONGREGATION:
We open our hearts in welcome. Be among us in hope, in joy and in our ongoing struggle to be a faithful people!

PASTOR AND NEW COMMUNITY MEMBERS:
Do you affirm the vows that you made or were made for you at the time of your baptism?
WE DO.
Do you claim the love of the Creating God as the rule in your lives?
WE DO.

With this community, will you claim the love and power of Jesus Christ over all things? Even over the power of nation-state, society and culture?

WE WILL.

With this community will you accept Jesus Christ as savior, Guide and Hope for your own lives in community?

WE WILL.

As ones entering this congregation, will you promise to be fully present with your gifts, talents and graces as a child of God? And will you promise to be fully present also with the resources at your disposal, both financial and material?

WE WILL.

Through the joys of being a Christian community, will you endeavor to love, struggle, forgive and grow as one with us?

WE WILL.

Will you affirm that the love we share as a community is stronger than our brokenness, more powerful than our weakness, and that it is in and through this love that we continue, persevere and move forward together in ministry?

WE SO AFFIRM.

And will you, as Christians, recall that our structures and institutions will need to be challenged and called into account, and will you promise to back up your gifts, talents, and grace with these challenges?

WE WILL.

With the promise of new life knocking at our door, and with your presence already adding to the loving power of this community, you are welcome! Come, be among us as ministers in the holy task!

THE CONGREGATION (*comes forward to lay hands on the new members*)

We rejoice to receive you as members of this faith community. As new members of this church, we will stand with you through the challenges and wonders of being in ministry together.

THE COMMISSIONING OF A MISSION DELEGATION

Dear friends, we are here together to celebrate, to bless and to send forth our friends and community members in the name of the Risen Christ. As we do this, the echoes of history wash over us and we recall our ancestors in the faith sending others before us. We believe that just as the Holy Spirit called Saul and Barnabus, St. Frances, Dorothy Day, and Frances McConnell, so too does the Spirit call these sisters and brothers before us today.

It is with deep joy and hope that we send *(list the names)* on an adventure of faith. We send them as emissaries, not only of our faith community, but also of the liberating love of God in Christ Jesus. We send them to establish a relationship between our community and the Church in (name of country).

As you go forth, this commission will strengthen our bond with you and our connection to the Church in (name of country). Remember that you go as partners in Christ, not as ones better. Remember that you go in love and humility, not with answers or solutions.

And remember that you bear the name of this body of Christ as you go.

THE BLESSING OF THE DELEGATION:

We praise You, O God, and give You our total allegiance. In You, we find our security, our hope, and our joy.

Bless, O God, these servants who go forth to build bridges and friendships with our sisters and brothers in (name of country). Fill their hearts with the power of Your Holy Spirit, and open their minds, their eyes, and their arms to the realities of the people they will meet.

We send them this day as messengers of peace in Your name, marked with the sign of the cross and anchored in Your humility and Your grace.

Bless the crosses we now give as a sign of Christ's love (*distribute crosses to each member of the delegation).*

THE CONGREGATION SENDS THE DELEGATION FORTH:

We the people of this church commission you to go in the name of hope and love, in the reality of the nonviolent, noncoercive Gospel to build a bridge over which many may travel, and across which the love of God may flow in both directions. Amen.

SOME THOUGHTS ABOUT MARRIAGE

As a pastor, I am witness to a virtual parade of people in and out of my office who want me to "perform" their weddings as though I were being hired as in actor in their private play. "Why," I ask each couple, "do you want to be married in a church? Why not a judge at City Hall?" Almost without exception, they look askance, and say something like, "Well, your church is pretty." Or, "Your church is close to where we're having the reception." Or at best, "My grandmother was a Methodist."

Most, in fact, nearly all who come to me about weddings have no formal relationship with the church. They don't attend or plan to attend worship or participate in the life of a Christian community. When asked what their religious affiliation is, many shrug and say, as though they're guessing on a test question in front of their fourth grade teacher: "Protestant? I think my mother was Protestant. Yeah. That's it. Protestant." And my favorite is the slightly indignant tone that enters the voice as the couple say, "We don't believe in organized religion, but we're VERY spiritual people, you know."

I have no statistics to support this, but it's my guess that many clergy find themselves "performing" weddings perhaps more than any other task. And I would suggest as we struggle to reclaim our heritage and our authenticity, that it is time to take a look at marriage.

Indeed, many churches are doing exactly that. Some clergy will not marry anyone who is not an active member of their congregation. Others, myself included, require extensive counseling and a minimum period of time attending the church. When I mention that they must join us in worship for a minimum of six weeks, the majority of couples decide that they'd like to look elsewhere for someone to "do" their wedding.

Why does the church involve itself in marriage?

Culturally, marriage harkens back more to property arrangements and family connections than it does to love and sacred union. While it retains a sacramental status in the Roman tradition, it seems that the blessing of marriages by the church is at least a bit odd. Add to this the fact that clergy are empowered by the state to marry people. How interesting! By accepting this largess from Caesar, do we imply that we would stop performing marriages if it became suddenly illegal?

In the church we marry people as a rite of the Christian community. It implies, and in most liturgies, states clearly that this covenant is "established by God." If so, shouldn't the people being married believe in God? Shouldn't the people partaking of a sacred covenant be an authentic part of the community, worshiping, giving, sacrificing and praising God?

If not, then why do we marry these people? Is the church so co-opted by culture that we have become a secular institution giving tacit nods to things like marriages, baptism, and yes, war?

Sadly, the answer is "yes." And I would suggest that each time a clergyperson does the bidding of the secular culture by marrying people who have no commitment to the faith, the church disappears a little more into the folds of what St. Paul would call "This World".

So I say to clergy and lay alike, when we marry, let it be in the context of the church and all that implies in terms of covenant, community and commitment. When we marry,let us borrow from our Roman cousins by letting it be a little sacramental in nature. And when we marry, let us take our own faith seriously, calling those we marry to take the vows, the Christian context, and the covenant, not as a good party, but as truly sacred.

What follows is a Service of Christian Marriage used at Washington Square United Methodinst Church on several occasions.

The form of the ceremony follows the order found in the United Methodist Hymnal. The rite itself is written by Schuyler Rhodes.

THE SACRED COVENANT OF MARRIAGE

THE PEOPLE OF GOD GATHER IN HOPE AND JOY

THE PRELUDE:

THE GREETING: The Pastor

Sisters and brothers, we gather today in worship to celebrate the covenant of marriage. For us, this is a powerful moment in that we are all present to support and nurture (name) _______ and (name)_______ as they begin a new life together rooted in love and partnership. This moment is powerful also because we ourselves are a covenant people. From the time of Moses to the New Covenant brought to us in the blood of our Savior, we have understood and defined ourselves as people who are committed and part of a sacred agreement. The covenant of marriage that we witness today is also established by God. It is an echo of the covenant that God made with us, and that we make with each other as a people of faith. For truly, we are God's people.

Marriage is represented for us in the Gospel where our Savior attended a wedding at Canna. We know, too, that Jesus referred to the coming "Kingdom" or Realm of God, comparing it to a wedding feast. He called himself the Bridegroom, telling parables full of the joy and completeness of the weddings, and we cannot but claim this as part of what we do here today.

Friends, just as the grace that God gives us in Christ Jesus is a new beginning, so too is this special covenant of marriage a new beginning for _______and_______.

TO WITNESS THE DECLARATION OF INTENT

PASTOR: (*to the persons who are to be married*)

_______and_______, few activities in life prosper without the discipline and clarity of ongoing intention and purposefulness. So it is that I ask you to publicly declare before God and this community your intention to enter into sacred covenant together, knowing that you do so as recipients of God's grace in Christ Jesus, who calls you to the same purposefulness you declared in your baptism.

(Name)_______, will you accept_______as your partner in the sacred covenant of marriage? Will you love (him) as (he) is, accepting him, comforting him, nurturing and nourishing (him) through illness and health through good times and bad, and making the choice of this covenant for your life, will you be faithful to (him) as long as you both shall live?

RESPONSE: I WILL.

PASTOR: (Name)_______, will you accept_______as your partner in the sacred covenant of marriage? Will you love (her) as (she) is, accepting (her), comforting (her), nurturing and nourishing (her) through illness and health, through good times and bad, and making the choice of this covenant for your life, will you be faithful to (her) as long as you both shall live?

RESPONSE: I WILL.

TO EXPRESS THE COMMITMENT OF THE COMMUNITY

In the joining of _______ and _______ we witness to and celebrate the creation of a new family. But this family does not exist alone. In the coming days, months and years, they will require the support and nurture of each one of you. They ask now, not only for your blessing and approval, but for your promise of support.

THE CONGREGATION: We celebrate the power and wonder of the covenant you make this day, and we pledge as individuals and community to be present for you during the good times and bad as friends, supporters and family. We pray that you will find your life together to be a blessing, and by God's grace we will be participants and observers of this Holy Union with you in the sight of our God.

PRAYER: The Pastor

Holy and Gracious Redeemer, once again we feel the honor of claiming You and Your love as the source of all power, security and goodness. Through You we find our common journey to faithfulness, knowing that You love us with a limitless power and claim us as Your own even as we stumble and fall along the way. We thank You for the sustaining power of Your Holy Spirit, O God, and stand together in joy as we experience Your presence in the making of this sacred partnership, through Jesus Christ our Savior, Redeemer, and our Rock, we pray, Amen.

TO RECEIVE THE WORD OF GOD

THE SHARING OF THE HOLY SCRIPTURE:

THE SERMON: The Pastor or other Worship Leader

MUSIC FOR MEDITATION UPON THE WORD:

INTERCESSORY PRAYER: The Pastor

Holy and Wonderful God, Creator and Lover of all people, we pray that You will shower Your blessings upon________ and _______ who come forward now to give the vows of marriage. Grant, Sacred Friend, that they may give and receive these promises in the power of Your love. Walk with them so that they may grow in wisdom, in peace and in love through all the days of their lives, struggling always to give to the world these same gifts that they receive in abundance through Your child Jesus, our Christ. It is in His name and in the power of Your Spirit that we pray this, Amen.

TO WITNESS THE MARRIAGE OF
_______and_______

THE EXCHANGE OF VOWS:

(Partner 1 to Partner 2) In the name of God, I, (name)_______
take you (name)_______in the sacred covenant of marriage.
From this day forward, I will hold you and help you.
I will you walk with you and be with you through it all.
In illness or health, in wealth or poverty,
in the good times and the bad
I will love and cherish you until we are parted by death.
This is my sacred vow.

(Partner 2 to Partner 1) In the name of God, I, (name)_______
take you (name)_______in the sacred covenant of marriage.
From this day forward, I will hold you and help you.
I will you walk with you and be with you through it all.
In illness or health, in wealth or poverty,
in the good times and the bad
I will love and cherish you until we are parted by death.
This is my sacred vow.

THE BLESSING AND EXCHANGE OF THE WEDDING RINGS:

Pastor: The circle is an ancient symbol which speaks to us of the unending love of God through the grace of our Savior Jesus Christ. For us, these rings signify that same love as it is expressed in the union of_________and_________in the covenant of marriage.
Bless O God, the giving of these rings and those who wear them, that they might partake of Your peace and live in the wonder of Your love all the days of their lives. Amen.

Partner 1:_______, I give you this ring as a symbol of my love and a sign of the promise I make this day. And with the whole of my being, I pledge myself to you as your life partner, and honor you among people as the one whom I have chosen. In the name of the Creator, the Word, and the Holy Spirit, so be it.
Partner 2:_______, I give you this ring as a symbol of my love and a sign of the promise I make this day. And with the whole of my being, I pledge myself to you as your life partner, and honor you among people as the one whom I have chosen. In the name of the Creator, the Word, and the Holy Spirit, so be it.

THE DECLARATION OF MARRIAGE: (The Pastor)

Today you have come here and declared your intentions to be married one to the other. Before God and this community you have exchanged sacred vows and given each other the symbols of these promises. I pray that God blesses your marriage and fills you both with an abundance of joy and new life.

(*to the people*) You have witnessed today these two given to each other by the sharing of vows and the exchange of rings. You have participated in this covenant and promised to nourish and support them in the new lives they have chosen.

Acknowledging this in hope and power I announce to you now that these two ARE joined as one, in the name of the Creating God, the Word become flesh, and the Power of the Holy Spirit, Amen.

TO SHARE THE BREAD AND THE CUP

THE INVITATION:

THE PRAYER OF GREAT THANKSGIVING: Here the community may celebrate the Eucharist with the couple. (See the Eucharistic prayers).

THE SHARING OF HOLY COMMUNION:

TO GO FORWARD IN JOY AND HOPE

MUSIC OF CELEBRATION: (A hymn or other appropriate music)

BLESSING & BENEDICTION: (*pastor to the couple*) May the love of God live in your hearts and reign in your lives together. Go now, giving yourselves to God, to the world, and to each other.

(*pastor to the people*) Know that you are also partners in this Holy Union. You are witnesses to God's love and you are friends, neighbors and family to these who have joined together today. As you go forward, may the grace of God in Christ Jesus go with you and live in your hearts giving you a peace beyond your understanding, now and always, Amen.

THE POSTLUDE:

A RITE FOR HOLY BAPTISM
FOR ADULT BAPTISM

Leader: In baptism, we put on the mantle of our Savior, taking the name of Christ and becoming one with His body, the Church. In this sacrament we are brought into union with God's ongoing act of salvation, and through water and the Holy Spirit, we are born anew. This is not a solitary act, or a rite of passage done outside of relationship to the community of faith. It is an act of community, a moment of solidarity, the beginning of a new reality rooted in the love of God in Christ Jesus.

People: Baptism is a bold pronouncement of a life-changing and society-challenging commitment.

Leader: It is a statement of values and ethics.

People: It is a commitment of love, vulnerability and peace.

Leader: It is the starting point for a new life rooted in Holy Scripture, and informed by tradition, reason and experience. Sister and brothers, in the power of the Holy Spirit and in the loving embrace of this community I present (name)_______ for baptism. *(The faith community comes forward, gathering in a circle around the candidate).* In the name of God and in front of these witnesses, I call upon you to respond to the following questions:

Leader: Do you renounce the forces of wickedness whether they be spiritual or social?

Response: I do.

Leader: Do you renounce your allegiance to this world and its understanding of power in favor of the power of God's world?

Response: What is the power of God's world?

Leader: The power of God's world is weakness to this world. The power of God's world is found in self-giving love and compassion. It is found in forgiveness and love of all people.

Response: I do renounce the power of the world and claim God's power as the power and motivation in my life.

Leader: Do you pledge yourself to an intentional life which will help you to turn away from brokenness and anger, from selfishness and sin?

Response: I do so pledge.

Leader: Do you embrace the reality and freedom of God's love?

Response: I do.

Leader: In the powerful liberation that comes with God's freely offered love, will you offer your energy and your life in resisting evil, injustice and oppression?

Response: I will.

Leader: Will you do this without yourself resorting or oppression?

Response: I will.

Leader: Do you confess that Jesus Christ is your Savior?

Response: I do.

Leader: Do you realize that in claiming Jesus Christ as Lord and Savior, you must reject all other lords and all other powers, including those of national and political governments, social categories and institutional hierarchies?

Response: I do.

Leader: Do you place your trust in God, promising to serve God in Christ in union with this church?

Response: I do.

(The Pastor addresses the Congregation and/or Sponsors)

Leader: Will you take it upon yourselves to be in relationship with these persons? Will you accept them just as they are? Will you love them? Nourish them? Laugh with them, cry with them and call them to account when it is necessary?

Response: I will.

Leader: Will you renew your commitment to be a witness, not only to these new members of the Body of Christ, but to a world in need of healing and love? Will you give your life as an example by which many may come to accept the freely given gift of God's grace?

Response: I will.

Leader: Let us join together in professing the Christian faith:

(Here may be said a classic confession such as the Apostles or Nicene Creed. Congregations are encouraged to develop their own confessions which speak to their ministry and faith journey while keeping the timeless commitment to the love of God in Christ.)

A PRAYER OF THANKSGIVING OVER THE WATER

Gracious and Wonderful God, we pause in the power of the Holy Spirit to gather with our ancestors in faith at the River Jordan. Today with John and Jesus we wade into the water, feeling the cleansing power of new life.

This is the same new life, O God, that spread over the waters in eons past, bringing light and life from darkness and nothingness. It is the same new life that lifted Noah above the floods. And it is the same new life that led the people through the Red Sea waters.

It is the same new life, Holy God, that came to us through the womb of Mary in the form of the one called Jesus.

This Jesus was baptized by John and anointed by Your Spirit, and He called His disciples as He calls us today to share in the new life of this baptism so that in our dying we might know new life, and in our rising we might be a light, even to the whole world.

God, whose name is love, whose substance is love, pour out your Holy Spirit on this water so that those who receive it now may feel the power of their sins break and wash away leaving only the final victory of new life in Your love.

We pray this as we stand with the Saints by the river, lifting our hearts to our Lord and Savior, Jesus the Christ, Amen.

(*The Candidates for Baptism come forward separately to receive the gift of water and spirit)*

(Name)_______I baptize thee in the name of the Creator, the Word, and the Holy Spirit, Amen.

(*Then the community of faith comes forward, laying hands on the newly baptized, saying*) May the power of the Holy Spirit live in you and provoke you to faithfulness as a follower of Christ Jesus, now and always, Amen.

RITE OF HOLY BAPTISM
FOR CHILDREN

THE PASTOR: Brothers and sisters, in the early Church, the rite of baptism was reserved for adults and those who chose with intention and purpose to claim Jesus Christ as the Sovereign Ruler of their hearts and their lives. The preparation for this life altering commitment was long and arduous, requiring discipline, patience, and persistence.

Today, we believe with our ancestors in faith, that in baptism we take on the mantle of Christ. With the Saints who have gone before, we too claim Jesus Christ and the love He brings as our way in this world. We know that today as then, this takes discipline and commitment. And we know, as we prepare to baptize these children before us, that we stand as partners with the Holy Trinity, joined as community, family, and friends in a sacred promise to raise these young people up into a living and powerful faith.

THE GATHERED COMMUNITY: We embrace the faith of our ancestors, and stand with them in the power of the Holy Spirit to commit ourselves as partners and members of the household of faith as we walk with these young people, guiding and caring for them as they grow in the faith.

THE PASTOR: My friends, I present (names)________, who are/is before us today to partake of this Holy Sacrament.

(*addressing the God Parents/Sponsors:*) On behalf of a Christian community committed to reclaiming the integrity and authenticity of the Church of Jesus Christ, I ask you: Do you reject all that is evil in this life?

SPONSORS: I DO.

THE PASTOR: Do you stand in the love of God in Christ Jesus, renouncing the power of this world and all its benefits?

SPONSORS: I DO.

THE PASTOR: Do you repent of your sin?

SPONSORS: I DO.

THE PASTOR: Do you accept the freely given grace of God and the power it gives you to resist evil, injustice, violence and oppression wherever and whenever you may encounter them?

SPONSORS: I DO.

THE PASTOR: Will you so resist, even with your life?

SPONSORS: I WILL.

THE PASTOR: Do you claim Jesus Christ as the Sovereign Ruler of your life? And do you promise to give your life in service to your Sovereign, working within the Church which is opened by Christ's own hand to all people regardless of nationality, race, ethnicity, gender or sexuality?

SPONSORS: I DO.

THE PASTOR: Will you accept the responsibility for nurturing these children (this child) in the faith? Will you teach them? Admonish them? Care for them? Will you live a life of intention and purpose, being an example to these children (this child) so that they might grow to accept Jesus Christ as their Sovereign in their own time and in their own hearts?

SPONSORS: I WILL.

THE PASTOR: *(to the congregation)***:** With those who stand before us today as sponsors for this baptism, will you renew your commitment to Christ?

CONGREGATION: WE WILL.

THE PASTOR: *(to the congregation)***:** Will you persist in your honest and lasting affection for each other? Will you be as family to (names)_______, surrounding them with love and support? And will you re-dedicate yourselves to lives of purpose and intent, being an example for these children (this child) so that they might grow with you into the faith which we claim?

CONGREGATION: WE WILL.

THE PASTOR: *(to the congregation)***:** Will you pray for them? Will you pray with them? Will you walk with them in a united spirit of patience and love so that together we may all be true disciples?

CONGREGATION: WE WILL.

THE PASTOR: Let us raise our voices in joy and celebration as we profess our faith: Do you believe in the Creating God, who made heaven and earth and all things that are?

CONGREGATION *(including sponsors)***:** WE DO.

THE PASTOR: Do you accept Jesus Christ as your Sovereign Lord?

CONGREGATION: We claim Jesus Christ
as our Savior and the Sovereign Ruler of our lives.
We know that for us, this Christ is God's own child,

born of the woman Mary.
We believe that, fully human and fully divine,
Jesus walked among us as the embodiment of God's love.
In the power and wonder of this love,
Jesus healed the sick, fed the hungry and liberated the oppressed,
proclaiming a new way of being which is free of coercion and domination,
free of violence and greed, free of the manipulative power of this world,
and full of the vulnerable, compassionate love of God.
We are witnesses to this love, and know that
it is this love which provoked political and religious authorities
into torturing and executing Jesus.
We know it is this love that also raised him up from the tomb
showing us that new life and resurrection belong to us as well.
We believe in this love, and commit our lives to living in its power.
In the name of God and in the love of Christ Jesus we speak these words,
Amen.

A PRAYER OF THANKSGIVING OVER THE WATER (*see page 98*)

STORIES: RECLAIMING AN ANCIENT TRADITION

Stories are an important part of who we are as a people. In a significant way, Holy Scripture is our story as much as it is the story of our ancestors in faith. But we have our own stories as well. Stories which speak to our spirit, our hope, and our identity. Stories are also excellent teachers. Jesus knew this, and used stories extensively in his teaching. To a degree, these stories are parabolic. They provide metaphors in which we can move, live and learn together.

After telling one of these stories during a stint as a guest preacher, an irate clergyman came to me demanding to know if the Uncle Ned stories were "true." I asked him if he thought that Jesus' parables were "true," and he seemed to become even more agitated.

After all these years, I shall answer my friend. "Yes." The stories are true. I didn't make these stories up myself. They've come to me at church suppers and clergy luncheons; at the fire hall and in my own office. But no matter where they originate, it seems clear that Uncle Ned lives! These stories have been embellished and changed over and over again, and they're still as true as they have always been.

Ned himself is a character. He is part my grandfather, and part the old kitchen boss in my first job as a grill cook at the Fish and Game Club. He's also partly made up of all the wonderful women and men that God has sent to me on my journey.

The name "Ned," belongs to the best friend of my youth, who has been lost to me in the folds of time. This "Ned" taught me the folly of not rooting for the Yankees. He taught me the wisdom of always carrying a loaded squirt gun through our neighborhood in June. And he was the first person ever to stick up for me in a fight.

In a way, Ned is the sage in all of us. He is a teacher in the same way that we are all teachers of each other. A listening, open presence, with ears to hear, and eyes to see. Ned is you. Ned is me.

UNCLE NED AND THE NEW SUIT

Ned wanted one thing. It was the blue suit in the window of the men's store down the street. He wanted it so badly that he could almost taste it. Week after week after week, he saved his meager earnings from his job sweeping out the local movie theatre until finally he had enough to purchase the object of his desire.

He walked into the store, pointed to the suit, and told the salesman, "I want that blue suit." The salesman, sensing a sure thing, grabbed the suit from the rack, the last one, and sent Ned into the changing room with it.

Before too long, Ned emerged. It was quite a sight. The sleeves on the jacket were easily three inches too short, and the legs on the pants looked as though poor Ned was expecting a flood.

With a disappointed smirk, he shrugged and said, "I guess it doesn't fit."

"Oh, no!" cried the salesman. "You couldn't be more wrong. This suit looks wonderful on you. In fact," he said with a sweep of his arm, "it is you."

Ned snorted, looked skeptical, and stammered, "I don't know..."

"Are you kidding?" the salesman shot back. "You look really sharp. Seriously now. I've seen lots of suits walk out of this place, but you look sharp!"

"But the sleeves," Ned exclaimed. "Look at the look at these pants! Everything's too short. It doesn't fit."

"Oh, but it does," cooed the salesman. "All you have to do is bend your legs a little bit at the knee." Ned tilted his head sideways and peered at the man as though he had lost his mind. "Go on. Try it. That's right. Now hunch your shoulders up like this."

Ned did as he was told, and with bent legs and shrugged shoulders, the sleeves and pant legs did indeed seem to come down a bit.

Smelling victory, the salesman pushed hard. "If you don't buy this suit, it'll be a crime."

Ned, still hunched over and bent at the knees trying to make the suit fit, reached for his wallet, unfolded it and paid the man.

As he left the store and started down the street wearing his new suit, people began to laugh at him. They'd point at him and shake their heads in disbelief. "Why would anyone go to such extremes simply to wear a suit?" Soon they stopped laughing at him and started ignoring him altogether. How could you take anyone seriously who was willing to contort themselves just to fit into a suit?

But Ned had paid for the suit, and he was going to wear it. Day after day, with his body twisted so the sleeves and pant legs would be the right length, he made his way to work and back home again.

After a while, his contorted form began to pain him. It was harder to move and he began to have cramps. He developed arthritis and had discomfort in his neck. Doctors told him, upon examination that his body was permanently deformed, and that he would not be able to walk again.

All from fitting his body into a suit that didn't fit.

UNCLE NED GOES FISHING

Uncle Ned loved to go fishing. No wonder. He was, apparently, quite good at it. Each time old Ned went fishing, he returned with a basket full to overflowing with slippery, and soon- to-be yummy, trout. We all grew up eating Uncle Ned's trout for Sunday dinner and telling stories about his prowess with a fly rod. It was something of a family legend.

All this was fine and good, except for cousin Al. Al, a tall fidgety man, was the county game warden, and owed his job to some distant relation on the side of the family that was decidedly not Ned's. Cousin Al was certain that there was something "fishy" about Ned's fishing. After all, he could never catch the limit on trout. Why could Ned? How did he do it? And in such a short time too. Usually his fishing expeditions would last only a few hours. And every time he'd come back with that annoying grin, showing off his basketful of trout. Al was determined to catch Ned in the act of doing something which almost certainly had to be illegal.

One day, Al decided to follow Ned. As Ned emerged from the barn with his fishing gear, he hugged the side of the house, as the noted angler slipped into the forest. After a walk of some thirty minutes, they came to the stream. Al was still at a discreet distance as Ned sat down on the bank of the creek and began to unpack his gear.

First the bait box. Nothing unusual there. Then a sandwich and thermos, and then that basket which always raised the hackles on Al's neck. But Al had to admit, it was only a basket. Nothing strange in that. And then, to his horror, Ned pulled a stick of dynamite from his bag. Puffing on his cigar, he calmly lit it, and tossed it into the stream. Moments later, a large explosion sent huge numbers of dead fish to the surface of the creek. Ned yawned, rose to his feet, waded into the water, where he began to fill his basket.

Al was thunderstruck. He couldn't believe what he had just witnessed. He had been sure that there was something funny going on, but this? Unbelievable. Recovering from his state of shock, he stumbled from the underbrush just as Al had returned to the grassy spot on the bank. "What do you think you're doing!" blurted the game warden. "You just can't go around blasting a public fishing stream! There are rules! There are laws against this! Family relationships aside, Ned, I'm just going to have to report this!"

As Al's tantrum raged, Ned calmly puffed on his cigar and reached down into his bag. Once again, his gnarled hand emerged with a stick of dynamite.

"Ned! You aren't listening to me! I want you to expain to me just what you think you're doing. How many hundreds of fish have you gotten in this way?"

Al kept fuming on about his duty and rules and such as Ned lit the second stick of dynamite. It fizzled rebelliously in Al's face as Ned handed it to him and grunted, "You gonna fish, or you gonna talk?"

UNCLE NED'S HUNTING STORY

Uncle Ned never shot anything in his life. That is, he never shot anything unless you count the sparrow he blew away at age twelve with his father's shotgun. He used to tell of walking over to pick up the remains with a quickly diminishing sense of power. It had a lasting effect. Nonetheless, Ned loved to hunt. He'd cradle the old gun under his arm each Saturday during hunting season and head off into the woods. The story 'round the dinner table was that he just loved to walk. The gun was the excuse. Sitting at the dinner table, our uninformed young minds wondered why we could walk all the time without the benefit of Grandpa's shot gun and Uncle Ned couldn't. But we were young, and grown-ups seemed to know what was happening.

One autumn day, when the air was crisp, and the sky was a deep crystal blue, Ned set out with his shot gun. As was his custom, he walked and thought, and thought and walked, losing all track of time and place. It wasn't too long, though, before he was brought out of his day dream by the fact that he was getting very thirsty. In fact, as Great Uncle Mike used to say, he was "parched." The only problem was that he had left his canteen on the kitchen counter right next to the sink where he had filled it.

Well, the next best thing would have to be a stream or spring. There must be one somewhere in these woods. Ned stopped, listening for the sound of running water. And sure enough, quietly, through the rustling of autumn leaves, he could hear the gentle gurgle of a stream somewhere up ahead. In a few moments he was there. He dropped his backpack and his gun and sprinted to the stream, putting his face down into the cool, crystal water and gulping down that wonderful crisp water. It tasted so good.

All of a sudden there was a snapping of twigs behind him and a loud roar. Startled and not a little afraid, he jumped up from the stream to see one of the biggest bears he had ever seen standing between him and his gun. Fear grabbed old Uncle Ned and he started shaking from head to foot. He didn't know what to do. If he made a quick movement, it might provoke an attack. On the other hand, if he stayed there, things didn't look too good either.

Not knowing what else to do, Ned shut his eyes tight and started to pray. He said, "Lord, I know You haven't seen too much of me in church lately. In fact, I know that, well, You may have a few issues You'd like to raise with me. All that's well and good, and I understand. But as You can see, I got a situation here, and I only want to ask You one thing, God. Please, let this be a Christian bear. Amen."

After this heartfelt prayer, Ned kept his eyes closed. He was too scared to open them, and too scared not to peek. So with a great amount of effort, he opened one eye and peered out at the bear.

And there, only a few feet from him, was the bear, on his knees with his paws pressed together. Both of Ned's eyes popped open in disbelief as the bear began to speak. In gravelly, but clear words, he said, "Dear Lord, I thank You for this food I am about to receive."

UNCLE NED GOES TO THE RECORD STORE

It was Cousin Alan's birthday. Not known for his attention to details such as birthdays, Uncle Ned had decided that this year, Al's birthday would be an exception. Not only that, he further determined that he would join the modern age and purchase cousin Alan one of those funny looking compact discs for his new stereo system. "After all," Ned mused, "he's going to be paying it off for the next ten years, he might as well have something to play on it."

Looking through the yellow pages, he came across a store called "Sam Goody's." Ned said it out loud a couple of times and concluded that it was a solid, trustworthy name, and that Sam could be counted on to give him what he wanted. So he wrote down the address and set out for his adventure at the record store.

In all this planning, however, Ned had not counted on one critical thing. It had been twenty-five years since he had been in a record store. In fact, the last time he had gone into a record store, there had still been records for sale.

Inside the store, Ned stood marveling at the spectacle. Posters, loud music, lots of people and CDs everywhere. There were thousands, no, maybe millions of them stretched row upon row across the huge store, broken down into categories he had never even heard of before. Hip Hop? Grunge? New Age? Whatever happened, Ned thought, to Elvis? The Platters?

After two hours of peering at hundreds of titles, Ned decided he had had it. It was time to talk to Sam.

Looking around the store, he saw a lot of young looking people wearing T-shirts that said "Sam Goody's." So he went up to one of them and tapped the young woman on the shoulder. "Where's Sam?" A silent, incredulous look came back at him. "I'm looking for Sam. Do you know where he is?" The woman stifled what seemed an awful lot like a giggle and said, "You want to see Sam?" "That's right," said Ned. "I'm having a horrible time finding what I want, and I thought Sam could give me a hand." "Well, Sam's not here," the young lady stammered. "In fact, I don't think he's ever been here."

Ned was flabbergasted. Never been there? He turned to the next "Sam Goody's" T-shirt and said, "Have you seen Sam?" The kid snorted and went on uncrating CDs. "Look. I'm not crazy. This is Sam's store, isn't it?" A cautious "yes" came back as the woman stepped discreetly a few feet away. "That's his name on the front of the store, isn't it?" Another cautious "yes" drifted his way. "Well, where is he? Do you mean to tell me that this is a store named after a guy, with his name all over it, and he's never been here?"

By this time the store security had come and was beginning to walk Ned to the door. Above the surging beat of the latest tunes and through the din of the crowd, Ned's voice could still be heard as they ushered him out. "Where's Sam Goody? What do you mean he's not here? Isn't that his name on your shirt? Isn't that his name out front? Where's Sam? Where's Sam?"

UNCLE NED GOES TO GREENWICH VILLAGE

All his life Ned had heard about Greenwich Village. This fabled neighborhood tucked away in the lower part of New York City's Manhattan Island held an almost mythic power for him. The corner of Bleecker and MacDougal, the fountain at Washington Square Park, and the cafes and coffeehouses that punctuate the urban landscape had become legend in his mind. One night, sitting at home over his instant cappuccino, he made up his mind that he would make the pilgrimage. He would go to Greenwich Village.

After raiding his savings account, making sure his sister would look after his dog, George, and finding someone to drive him to the airport, the plans were complete. It was really happening. He was so excited he could barely stand it. Greenwich Village. Images of poets with dark glasses and berets filled his mind. Pictures of poetry readings and groups of artists painting in the streets danced in front of him all night before he left.

At the airport Ned decided to take a taxi into the big city. As he slid in the back seat with his suitcase he said, "Take me to Greenwich Village." The driver grunted, and lurched out of the airport into traffic. Ned's heart was soaring. "How often," he mused almost out loud, "does someone get to do something they've always wanted to do?"

All of the sudden the cab pulled over to the curb. "This OK?" the driver muttered. A bit taken aback, and not wanting to appear that he didn't know where he was, Ned said, "Sure. Yeah. This is great. Perfect." And with that he was by himself on the street.

His first impulse was to find a cafe and have a double espresso, but first he'd better get his bearings. This didn't look like Greenwich Village. Where were the poets? The guitar players on the corner? And where were all those great jazz clubs? This couldn't be The Village. All Ned could see were the drug dealers displaying the benefits of a free market economy. That taxi driver probably didn't want to go to Greenwich Village and just dropped him someplace. But where? Where on earth was he? This couldn't be The Village.

As he began walking, he came to a man who looked like he should know, so Ned stopped him. “Excuse me, but I’m looking for Greenwich Village. Could you point me in the right direction?” The man smiled and shook his head muttering something about New Jersey, and said, “This is The Village. You’re smack in the middle of it.” “You’re kidding,” said Ned. “This is Greenwich Village? Are you sure?” The man chuckled and said, “I ought to be, I’ve lived here for the last five years.” “But how could this be— ” The man cut him off and said, “I promise, this is Greenwich Village. Now I have to go.” And with that he turned and walked away.

Ned was baffled. Something was wrong. Maybe he should ask someone else. But the next person he came to gave him the same reply, as did the next and the next. Each one insisted that in fact, Ned was standing in the middle of Greenwich Village. But for all the world, Ned couldn’t believe it. This wasn’t what he expected, what he had read of and dreamt about all these years. This couldn’t be Greenwich Village. He stamped his foot and started walking again. Sooner or later he’d find someone who would tell him where he should go to find Greenwich Village. Whatever it took, he’d find someone.